AN INDIAN JOURNAL

An Indian Journal

written and illustrated

by

NICHOLAS GARLAND

1983
The Salamander Press
Edinburgh

The Salamander Press Edinburgh Ltd
34 Shandwick Place, Edinburgh EH2 4RT

ISBN 0 907540 38 4
First published October 1983

Printed & made in Great Britain
Set in VIP Plantin
by Fakenham Photosetting Ltd, Fakenham, Norfolk
Printed by Spottiswoode Ballantyne Ltd
Colchester and London
Edited and designed by Tom Fenton,
Jennifer Law & Caroline Lawrence at the Salamander Press

To Caroline

Foreword

Sometime in the middle of 1981 Nick Garland came and asked me somewhat diffidently if we might be willing to let him off duty for a fortnight or so to visit Russia. He had never crossed the Iron Curtain; and he put the idea diffidently because cartoonists are not encouraged to travel like foreign correspondents. They are expected to draw their inspiration from the national scene (which at certain close seasons must severely test their inspiration).

We discussed the idea, not as an assignment for the *Daily Telegraph* but rather as a breath of fresh—well, different—air for him. It might be a good idea, we agreed grandiloquently, for him to broaden his horizon.

Nick Garland went off and, quite unexpectedly, kept a journal of his travels. He also made some sketches. What surprised us on his return was not the sketches, which we had come to take for granted, but the journal. It was written in the style of a letter home. The Victorians were very good at that kind of thing. There has not been much of it since.

Our sister ship, the *Sunday Telegraph*, thought well enough of it to publish excerpts—which we, for reasons of space, could not afford.

A year later Nick Garland proposed a visit to India. He had never visited the Third World. Again, we agreed the same terms; that is to say the journey would be undertaken without commitment. A cartoonist expected to produce at short notice his own comment on the public or political scene is entitled to break the chain to his drawing board once in a while and take a look at another part of the world.

His writing pen sharpened by experiences in the Soviet Union, Nick Garland wrote another journal. John Thompson, editor of the *Sunday Telegraph*, again thought highly enough of it to publish a portion. This book gives it all.

Nick Garland, though I have up to now concealed this from him, is a fortunate individual. A lot of people possess one professional discipline in this life. They can write, or play music, or draw. Not so many can manage two disciplines. We know that Nick can draw. What we have discovered from occasional pieces he has written for us over the years is that he can also write. Readers of this book can now discover that for themselves.

WILLIAM DEEDES *The Daily Telegraph*

Contents

Delhi
Jaipur
Agra
Nagpur
Calcutta

Delhi

Monday 15th November

The flight from London to Delhi was calm and easy. The plane was full of Indians. Scores of beautiful children. One family had three upwardly nubile little girls all speaking with strong clear American accents. The old couple sitting next to me were from Delhi and had been visiting their three children in the U.S.A., one of whom was a doctor, one an engineer and the other an endocrinologist. The old lady was very fat and kept clambering over me and spilling out of her sari, which seemed to amuse her husband; he later went and sat somewhere else so that she could stretch out over two seats.

Over Russia and Afghanistan I looked out to see what I could see but we were flying high over thick cloud.

My first impression of Delhi airport was of its general seediness. It was a friendly sort of tattiness, not filthy or unpleasant at all. Getting through Immigration Control took quite a while but I was content to stand and queue and even took a kind of pleasure in watching the officials staring at bits of paper and taking notes and moving very slowly to confer with each other; and I also enjoyed noting the strangely haphazard way that now and then a family or individual would be let through. My turn finally came and the solemn official looked at my passport and landing card for a while then put it down and wandered away. So I picked it up and went through without waiting for him to return.

I asked a uniformed man how to get to my hotel. He smiled and waved me towards a door. Through it I found myself in a street full of stationary cars. I asked a driver, 'Are you a taxi?' 'No,' he said. He smiled too.

Three young men came up to me in a brisk businesslike way. 'Where are you going?' 'The Oberoi.' 'O.K.' A car appeared and they all made to get in. One took my bag. 'How much?' I wanted to know. One said a certain number of rupees. 'I haven't any rupees, only pounds.' 'Only what?' 'Pounds—sterling.' 'Oh,' he did a lightning sum: 'ten pounds.' 'I haven't got ten pounds,' I lied. 'How much have you got?' I had some loose notes in my pocket. 'Five pounds or six pounds,' I said, 'I'm not sure.' 'Six then,' he said. I got in.

The drive was boring. The streets empty. There was very little to let you know where you were. Wide tree-lined ways with roundabouts, a few low buildings. Once I saw a cow lying uncomfortably on the shoulder of the road and once a man lying even more uncomfortably on the raised centre division of the four-lane highway.

Eventually after a fifteen-minute drive, during which I was asked if I wanted the taxi again to go to Agra perhaps or anything else, we arrived at the huge modern hotel. I got out and gave the man five pounds. 'There's five,' I said. 'Six?' he said hopefully. 'Sorry, that's all I've got.' He seemed quite content. I took his name and phone number in case I needed it.

I checked in and changed some money and was taken up to my room. It is comfortable and clean and has a fridge with soft drinks in it, two of which I drank right away. Then I rang home. I got through almost at once and heard Alexander's 'Hello Dad!' It was lovely and quite crazy to think I could be so far away and yet so easily be able to get in touch. I am truly a child of the thirties: modern jet travel and communications fill me with wonder and surprise.

I felt restless and after lying on my bed for a while decided to go for a stroll.

Little lights were burning in the foyer because tonight is Diwali. A beautifully uniformed and turbanned man opened the door for me and I stepped out into the warm night. It was about one thirty in the morning. I was in the hotel grounds and couldn't easily see where to go. One direction looked as if it might lead to a garden. I passed beneath some trees and ahead of me saw two figures armed with what looked like pick handles. One of them turned towards me; the other rested against a wall. I casually changed direction, stepped over a low wall and followed another path that brought me back towards the hotel. I turned left and arrived at a sort of back entrance near a car park. I paused and a well-dressed, well-spoken, and handsome young man said, 'Can I help you sir?' 'No, it's okay, thanks.' He walked over to a group of chairs near a closed gate and sat down. Then I noticed more men holding staves. One or two looked as if they were in uniform.

I walked over to the young man whose name, I learned later, was Rattan. 'Perhaps you *can* help me,' I said. He looked up politely. Round his neck were earphones, and a small tape deck was in his hand. 'May I sit down for a minute?' 'Sure.' In a few moments he explained that he was a trainee at the hotel, one of thirty-six male and female trainees, and he had been put on sentry duty for the last few nights because a workers' dispute, over someone claiming wrongful dismissal, had resulted in a series of night attacks on the hotel. Hence the armed men I'd seen patrolling earlier, and hence this lot here.

'They came and threw some rocks at the hotel the other night so we've hired these chaps.'

'Where did you hire them from—I mean what do they do when they are not doing this?'

'They come from agencies—police—sort of detective agencies.'

'Would they use these clubs of theirs?'

'Oh yes, certainly. If they had to.'

We were joined by Rajat, one of Rattan's colleagues. They were charming and friendly, utterly relaxed and goodnatured. We chatted about England. They'd heard all about the Brixton and Toxteth riots.

Suddenly there was a loud bang and a flash and a rocket

whizzed over our heads towards the hotel. The two young men turned mildly to see where the fireworks were coming from. The guards hardly bothered to look up. Several of them were asleep on the ground nearby.

'It's them,' said Rattan.

'The strikers?' I asked.

'Well they're not really strikers—they've been suspended on half-pay pending an inquiry. One of them has been accused of fraud.'

'Who is doing their work then?' I asked.

'Oh, other workers.'

'Does that make them (I indicated the firework party) angry?'

'Yes. We have to give the new workers police protection if they leave the hotel, but we've given them rooms in the hotel.'

The bangs and rockets continued to go off. Rattan telephoned someone. He had a field telephone on a chair. He explained to me that if one of the guests complained to the police the police would be round fast and sort out the demonstrators. He laughed. 'It's better if it comes from a foreigner,' he said.

We walked over to the gate and could see two men behind a hedge across the road lighting bangers with glowing cigarette ends. A guard went over to them. I asked them what he was saying.

'He's saying, "What do you think you're doing?" They are saying they are celebrating Diwali. So now he is saying, "Well go and do it somewhere else."'

Gradually and grudgingly, letting off a rocket or two towards us as they went, the two men withdrew and the warm night became quiet again.

This whole scene happened with a dream-like serenity. The bangs were loud but no one raised a voice or moved hurriedly. No one did anything very much. Rattan and Rajat watched, bored and patient, neither angry nor contemptuous. In the middle of it all Rajat wanted to have a go on Rattan's earphones but it proved too complicated to unwire them all.

Soon, feeling tired, I said I was going to bed. They both stood up and shook hands and smiled and said they hoped we'd meet again.

Tuesday 16th November

I woke late: it was about 10.00. I opened the curtains and looked out. My room is on the eighth floor and the view is wide. It was a clear hot day and several large kites or buzzards floated in the sky. A faint haze filled the air and far away over the trees I could see the tall buildings and occasional dome of central Delhi. Even high up in my room I could hear the roar of traffic. I wished I had woken earlier. The day looked promising and I was sorry to have missed any of it.

I put on the lightest clothes I had, put a sketch book and guide book in my satchel and went down the stairs. In the lobby of this very grand hotel (too grand really to have any charm or local colour) I saw a sign saying 'Buffet'. So I went in and had some excellent coffee and to my surprise, croissants. I don't know what I was expecting: dal on toast and curried porridge perhaps, but I wasn't expecting croissants.

I ate quickly and walked out into the open air. It was hot; not savagely hot; bordering on the too hot. It was excitingly hot; exotically hot. There was a row of taxis and I got in the first one. The driver wore a turban so I assume he was a Sikh. I said 'Connaught Place please.' 'Where?' 'Connaught Place—where the Janpath joins Connaught Place.' 'Are you going shopping?' 'Yes, and looking around.' 'I can show you around,' he said.

We set off. He honked his horn at everything that moved and everything he thought might move. He didn't drive fast, simply extraordinarily dangerously. He overtook, he barely squeezed past other vehicles, he left braking until the last possible moment, he swerved and kept up a continual and more or less incomprehensible chatter. 'That's Parliament building down there.' He pointed at some trees. 'I can show you Parliament building, ambassador's house, office blocks quite high, lots of things.'

'Where are we going at the moment?' I asked, wondering whether I was already on the proposed tour. I didn't catch his reply. The traffic was not heavy but very noisy; everyone peeped all the time, and drove madly but not apparently very bad-temperedly. It's difficult to describe the dusty scene. I saw lots of trees and low buildings that were hard to identify; some could have been abandoned offices built years and years ago but there seemed to be people living in them; there might be washing hanging out, or one or two children standing around.

'What's this place?' I asked as we passed one such crumbling building.

'Oh, that!' the driver replied enigmatically. As we approached the centre the streets became more crowded. There were many cyclists and lambrettas. I was struck by the way girls rode pillion on the motor-scooters, gracefully sitting sidesaddle with their saris remaining neat and in place in spite of the slip-stream. Sometimes the driver of a scooter had a child up front while his wife casually held a baby behind, a sight to give an English traffic cop heart failure.

I began to see shops and offices and knew we must be near the centre. Suddenly the driver swung off the road into a car park below a building.

'What's this?'

'Very good shopping,' he told me.

'Is this Connaught Place?'

'Yes.'

'O.K. How much?'

'Nine rupees,' he said, 'that's not counting the extra.'

I'd been warned about this. 'What extra?' I said warily.

'Well, you see the meter is very old.' My guide book (the excellent *India, a Travel Survival Kit* published by Lonely Planet) had said that's what he'd say.

'Here's nine,' I said, without waiting for him to explain further.

'No, no need,' he said, refusing the money, 'I'll wait.' He

obviously hadn't abandoned all hope of the parliamentary tour. 'No extra charge,' he said. 'Come back in an hour or half an hour and I'll take you wherever you want to go.'

I agreed. I wanted first of all to find out where I was. I got out of the car and walked towards what looked like a shopping arcade the other side of the car park. My driver shadowed me. I was in a shopping arcade but not the one I was actually looking for. Out on the street my Sikh hovered nervously. I asked him if he knew the Government Handcraft Emporium. It was very near. Once more I got out and this time gave him ten rupees.

'No,' he said, 'I'll wait.' But I'd had enough of him. 'No extra charge—only five rupees,' he said.

'Well,' I said kindly, 'if you're still here when I get back.' He looked at me wearily.

All round Connaught Place, the huge circus at the centre of Delhi, are hundreds of shops selling mostly clothes and jewellery and art work of various kinds; paintings, carvings, little boxes, brass work and so on. There are also street merchants selling flutes and gewgaws: odds and ends, little padlocks in the shape of animals for instance. A man selling these came up to me. 'Look, look sir!'

'No thanks.'

'Just look—I put in the key . . .' He demonstrated the little lock. 'I have tiger, dog, deer . . .'

'No thanks.'

'Only one hundred rupees.'

'No, really, thanks.'

'All right fifty—that's very cheap. Don't you like them? Look at the tiger.'

I walked on.

'I'll give it to you for twenty—ten—take two for fifteen,' he said, pleading with me.

I felt irritated and sorry for him, and walked on. The sun was hot, the shaded shopping arcades were cool. The pavements were crowded and colourful, the traffic noisy. Braced for hordes of cringing, whining beggars, I saw only two or three all day who only sat and gestured gently if they caught my eye.

Ready for reeking filth everywhere, I saw only the sort of urban dirt you get in any big city; less litter than London and no graffiti, that curse of our towns. What I was unprepared for was the special sort of charm the place has. I think it may wear off pretty soon but at first everyone seems so helpful and courteous and the people are so good-looking. There is such a wild variation of costume and type. It often seems in a Western city street that all the people are living entirely separate lives, locked, by habit as much as anything else, into a withdrawn and isolated existence. From time to time in London you may share a moment with a stranger: you may smile together at a child's naughtiness or grimace sympathetically at an incident you've both noticed; you may accidentally touch someone and say 'sorry', but that's about it. Here in the jostling crowd people held hands, shouted, accosted each other, stopped and argued. When I was drawing, the little groups that formed to watch chatted interestedly together. It was impossible not to be stimulated by the energy of the scene. I'm sure one would quickly weary of over-solicitous shopkeepers urging you to buy their rubbish, but what a welcome change from those miserable English and French shopowners who are apparently enraged by your merely entering their shop, and who take a real pleasure in saying they haven't got whatever it is you're looking for.

There were very obviously poor people, and some who looked aimless, but they didn't necessarily look unhappy. Down a narrow alley off a main street I saw a hole or ledge let into the wall. In it squatted a man in a red turban while another sat by him preparing some food on a tiny fire. As I passed, the second man handed the first a bit of chapatti. They were talking quietly together and looked extremely relaxed and comfortable. The alley was dirty with pools of water here and there; cars squeezed down it sometimes and people picked their way past constantly; but the two men, in spite of the appalling squalor all round them, looked for the moment anyway completely at ease.

I frequently saw Europeans. Many were young boys and girls in their twenties, dressed in Indian clothes, carrying bright little bags round their necks and with idiotic more-Indian-than-thou expressions on their faces. They looked very much less Indian than they hoped. Like ageing swingers in jeans, their costumes had precisely the opposite effect to the one intended, serving only to signal that they wished to be something that they were not. I was amused to find that they brought out the skinhead in me here, just as they do floating around London.

I bought some odds and ends: two beautiful wooden toys made, I was told, by children. They are carved in the form of women who spin round throwing out their arms when you pull a string.

I stopped to draw now and then, each time attracting a small, good-natured crowd who answered my questions and sometimes praised my drawing.

Imperial Hotel, Delhi

I was on the lookout for two hotels that I knew were in this neighbourhood. One because a friend, Richard E, might be staying there; the other because, for complicated reasons, I was expecting a message to be left there. As I walked I suddenly saw the first hotel, the Imperial, which stood down a short, shaded drive off the main road. I walked past a saluting guard. Richard was not there but I thought I'd look for a bar. It was about 2.30

by now and I was thirsty. Feeling the wonderful confidence that only a journalist on generous expenses feels, I strolled through the magnificent hotel and out onto a stone patio where an enchanting sight lay before me. I saw a wide beautifully-cut lawn bordered neatly with trimmed, flowering shrubs and bushes and partially shaded by tall trees. Across the lawn snaked a hosepipe. Bright umbrellas shaded half a dozen tables that were haphazardly placed on the grass. Each table had a pale green checked cloth. Waiters in high turbans and white tunics were serving food and drink to ladies and gentlemen sitting on brilliant white cane chairs. A black cat was playing by one group and being fed titbits by a slender lady; and up above the trees, birds of prey circled through the blue sky.

I sat by the edge of the lawn under a tree and ordered beer and samosas. I sat for an hour or so in the shade and watched this scene from the olden days. The heat and perhaps the beer made me feel slightly tipsy, adding rich fantasies to my already overloaded brain. A woman called out 'Boy' to a waiter, who instantly hurried to her side. I felt deliciously angry with her for being so rude, with him for being so humble, and grateful to both of them for playing their parts so perfectly. The afternoon drifted on and I left after getting directions to the other hotel.

I saw a marvellous road sign warning against careless digging that may sever telephone wires. (Like everyone, I thought I could more or less make India's notorious telephones more or less work—in fact, I more or less can't, and if I ever get through the party I want is not in. Out of perhaps two dozen calls I have actually spoken to only two of my contacts so far.)

After a few hundred yards in spite of my instructions I got lost. Incidentally, when I asked the girl at the Imperial for directions to the Centre Court Hotel, she asked a colleague something in Hindi, and held a longish conversation with him. Then she repeated his directions to me in English, adding at the end 'Anyone will know!'

I smiled at her. 'You didn't,' I joked. Her pretty face fell slightly. I raised my eyebrows to show I was only fooling but she pouted and fiddled with papers. I felt silly.

Janpath, Delhi

Once lost, I struck off down a dirty little side street and saw a cooking stall set in a cul-de-sac. It was built out into the road, if it could be called a road, and covered with swags of cloth, perhaps canvas. Under the canvas cooking pots bubbled and smoke rose. At least ten men and boys seemed to be in charge of it and it also appeared to be built across the entrance to a printing or photostating establishment. I stopped to draw it. As I closed my book, one of the watching crowd said, 'Are you drawing our office?' indicating a travel agency next door to the stall. 'No,' I said, 'I am drawing the men cooking.' 'Never mind,' he said. 'Please come inside. My boss would like to see you. Have a cup of tea.' He led me into his office, a travel agency, and sat down behind the counter. I sat in front. Another young man was sitting there and the three of us made polite conversation. After they had found out what I was doing in their city, they told me that they thought India was misrepresented in the European press.

'There is too much emphasis on poverty and hardship, not enough on India's achievements.'

The same thought was conveyed to me by the young hotel trainees last night and seems a genuine expression of pride in their country and a proper desire to see its better sides understood and known. I tried to cheer them up and said there were many commentators who knew India well and loved India dearly. I thought of James Cameron.

The tea came from the frighteningly unhygienic-looking establishment I had been drawing, brought in by a small boy. I thought 'Oh God', as I looked at its scummy surface where milky stuff floated turgidly about. I touched the cup; it was quite warm.

'Please drink,' they said. I noticed they didn't have any. I sipped. It was very, very sweet. I tried to ignore it and we talked animatedly for some time. At last one boy said, 'You don't like your tea. It's too sweet?' I answered him vaguely; and soon afterwards some Coca Cola came and more tea for them.

Foodstall near Janpath, Delhi

They were intelligent, impressive young men with beautiful manners. They answered all my questions and questioned me in turn. 'Were not the British people offended by their money being spent on Prince Charles's lavish wedding?' I told them that as far as I knew that was Charles's own dough. They asked about press freedom, praising the B.B.C. and British newspapers.

I heard a commotion outside. A beggar was squatting by the cooking stall surrounded by laughing, chatting men and boys. I couldn't tell what their attitude to the beggar was. Although from time to time one would hand him a coin or glass of tea, the rest milled about occasionally making exaggerated movements to avoid being touched by the beggar.

I asked what was going on.

'Oh! They are helping him.'

'They look as if they are teasing him.'

'Oh, no, he is retarded. They know him.'

'Is he often here?'

'Oh, yes, all the time.'

The young men had joined me by the glass door and smiled indulgently at the scene. Suddenly, and I mean suddenly, the door burst open and several extraordinary figures made as if to come into the office. They were thin, dark, raucous females, dressed outrageously in brightly coloured saris that somehow exposed a great deal of tummy and back and even leg. Several had rings in their noses and flowers in their hair. The young men spoke firmly to them and hurried them outside where they arranged themselves on the ground near the food stall. The cooks immediately began to serve them food, talking and joking with them. The beggar moved away. The half-a-dozen or so wild young women created a scene of magnificent dottiness. All their gestures seemed exaggerated and absurd as if they were being ironic or were unhinged. The young man left with me said, 'Homosexuals—eunuchs.'

I remembered the scene in Ruth Prawer Jhabvala's *Heat and Dust* where such troops of homosexuals or eunuchs are described. The Hindu word for them is *hijra*. The young men told me, 'They are good at dancing and entertaining. During Diwali or at wedding parties they come. They hear what is going on. They live in their own communities outside Delhi and each group has its own territory to work in. They do not trespass on each other's places of work. When they hear that a *hijra* has been born they will go and take the baby and bring it up with them in their own community.'

I interrupted. 'How do they know when a *hijra* is born?'

'Oh, they are well connected, they hear, perhaps the doctor tells them.'

'How can they tell a new born baby is a *hijra*?'

'Oh, they know, they can tell.'

'Are they beggars?'

'No; entertainers, dancers, singers.'

'But your friend has given them money?'

I could not understand his answer to this but it seemed that last night they had danced for Diwali and were now being paid.

'Oh, yes, he is giving them money,' he laughed, 'otherwise they may naked themselves.'

'What?'

'Naked themselves—to show disrespect.'

Hijra, Delhi

I watched the *hijra* eating and chattering. They were showing off a little, very self-conscious. It was as if they were in a state of constant 'flirt'. They looked extremely exotic and strange. I did a sketchy drawing of them but entirely failed to capture their look of abandoned, laughing confidence.

I met another young colleague of my two friends who turned out to be their boss. He was a journalist, albeit part-time. He worked for a Norwegian paper and knew one or two *Daily Telegraph* men. He tried to locate a journalist I'd been looking for on the hopeless telephone system. He failed too, but said if I could meet him here at 1.00 on Friday we'd go and meet some Indian cartoonists.

The people who said Delhi was a bore and told me not to waste time in Delhi were wrong. I could happily spend weeks here.

Eventually I continued my search for the Central Court Hotel and with the help of my travel agency acquaintances soon located it. It looked pretty crummy and I was fairly glad I had not finished up staying there. Upstairs I found a reception desk where to my surprise there was a message for me. Richard had said he'd get me a ticket to Simla so that I could go with him and Serena, who was accompanying him, when they went there. His letter told me he'd been unable to get me a ticket because he did not have my passport, but he told me how I could get one. It all sounded unbelievably complicated and I think I decided there and then I'd skip Simla. Delhi seemed so big and promising. I had so many people to continue to try to contact, I'm hopeless at arranging things, and was anyway quite happy to find out more about where I was and not rush on to somewhere new. And I'm lazy.

The afternoon was drawing in. I decided to go back to my hotel and try to fix a date for dinner. All day I had been badgered by the drivers of little rickshaws made out of converted mopeds, but now I couldn't see one. I walked for a bit looking around. I saw a tremendous argument going on. Two men were shrieking at each other in the presence of a stony-faced policeman who looked like Frank Finlay. His eyes swivelled now and then to glance with baleful contempt at one or the other of the furious men, and a large crowd looked on with intense interest.

I asked a Sikh, whom I hoped would be the driver of one of the several empty motorised rickshaws parked nearby, what was going on. He muttered something I didn't catch and turned away from me, so I never found out. I hailed a passing rickshaw. The Sikh driver glared at me.

'Oberoi Hotel.'

'Siddown,' he grunted.

The drive was sheer pleasure. Someone had said to me before I came, 'You might risk a ride in one of the motorised rickshaws. They always look as if they'll tip over but I've never heard of one doing so. They do crash sometimes I suppose and they really throw you about.' Consequently I was mildly excited at the prospect of the ride. I'd seen so many and they looked like such fun.

Rajat had told me the previous night that his elderly aunt had come to visit him recently and they had found themselves at a loose end. She had said, 'Let's go for a ride in an auto-rickshaw!' so they had, and she'd thoroughly enjoyed it. Not more than I was though, I bet. It was exactly like bumper cars, mercifully without the actual bumps, but it was touch and go. The driver overtook inside and out, peep-peeping. His face which I could see in the mirror was set and grim. Swerving, never braking, never pausing; red lights and pedestrian crossings bored him to death. He ignored them. At last we clattered up to the magnificent Hotel Oberoi.

'How much?'

'Ten rupees.'

'Ten rupees?'

'Yes.' He made an idiotic show of examining the meter which was covered with a piece of canvas.

'Ten rupees,' I said laughing, 'is more than the taxi cost this morning.'

'Taxi?' he said. 'What taxi?'

'The taxi I took this morning,' I explained.
'Ten rupees,' he said.
'Five,' I insisted, holding out a five note.
'Oh well,' he said, crumbling, 'whatever you want.'
I'm rather ashamed to say I gave him ten, I had enjoyed the whole thing so much.

Oberoi Hotel, Delhi

Up in my hotel room I began to telephone the contacts I had been given. I had no luck. Once or twice I got the ringing tone but no one answered. I actually got through to one number but my contact was out. I was told politely that I could call back at 8.30. I was starving hungry and thirsty. In the end, I just couldn't bear to go on making futile phone calls. I tried to get the hotel operator to phone for me. After a while she said, 'You must call 7–1, then hang up, pick up the phone, dial 0 and then your number. You are still connected, of course you cannot get through anywhere.' This ludicrous procedure seemed to work. I got a few ringing tones but still no answers, so I went to the bar and had a whisky. I was too exhausted to be quite sure, but it seemed to cost about fifty pounds and it was a small one.

I went to look at a Chinese restaurant on the roof, but it seemed silly to have a Chinese dinner in Delhi on my first night. I walked up and down the patio outside the restaurant looking at the superb view. The night was velvety dark, without stars or moon, and very warm. From all over the city, silent rockets rose into the sky and burst with little showers of silver glitter and later the sound of a distant pop was sometimes audible. I could hear, but not see, passing traffic.

I went downstairs and had dinner by myself. It occurred to me that the equivalent in London of what I have done today would be to have taken a taxi ride to Piccadilly from Highgate, and to have walked in an area from Trafalgar Square to Tottenham Court Road and back by Oxford Street and Soho to Piccadilly again.

Wednesday 17th November

Exhausted though I was I could not sleep last night. Perhaps it was excitement, perhaps jet lag. I don't know. I took a sleeping pill in the end and that worked. I was awoken at about 9.00 by the telephone. It was Richard calling. He said that of course I could get a ticket to Simla. He'd meet me at Baroda House where it was all done and we could do my train journey to Rajasthan, Nagpur and Calcutta at the same time. Richard has a kind of confidence and knowhow about him and the idea of getting help with my tickets changed everything. We arranged to meet at 10.00 at Baroda House. I had breakfast downstairs and took a taxi. I tried to prepare myself for a brush with the famous Indian bureaucracy.

There was no queue in the Tourist Office to which I was directed when we arrived. I explained to a patient, but not terrifically helpful woman at a desk what I wanted. She rattled away explaining about filling in forms and taking them here and there, and telegrams and so on, but I went numb with horror. It was rather like being at school listening to a teacher explaining something and realising you haven't grasped the first important point that is vital to all further comprehension. At school you could always try looking intelligent and attentive and just pray teacher didn't ask you anything; now, here, that would not do. On the other hand there was Richard. He arrived very soon and began going over it for me again. First I tried to work out an itinerary. It was obvious at once that I could not possibly go to Simla and all the other places *and* see anyone in Delhi. To cut a long story short, I decided not to go to Simla. Seeing that was what he was there for, Richard took this heavy blow very well. I began making out forms. I was hoping to visit Agra, Jaipur, Udaipur, Aurangabad, Nagpur and to finish up in Calcutta. Each leg of this journey needed its own form filled out twice. Having done that I took them to join the longish queue that had formed. Most of the people in the queue were young Europeans in various kinds of Indian dress. All were exceptionally plain and oddly irritating. They were being self-consciously calm and passive and even though that was the only sensible thing to do being sensible can be just as maddening as being silly. More maddening as a matter of fact.

When my turn came the lady said that what I needed was an Indrail Pass, but the man who issued them was not there. Where was he? Well he might be back at 2.30. Might be? It

Tourist office, Baroda House, Delhi

Booking clerk, Baroda House

would be prudent to telephone first to check. I was not feeling either calm or passive at this point. She was though. She tore off a bit of one of my forms and said, 'I can issue this.' I felt my carefully prepared collection of forms was no longer intact. It turned out I had to take the bit she had left me to another office the other side of town. I began to be glad I'd read Naipaul before coming here and tried to behave calmly. It was hot and I was sweating. Richard was at my elbow.

'Come on,' he said. 'That's it.'

I allowed myself to be led away.

He explained, 'We'll go and have lunch then you'll come back, get your Indrail Pass and I'll show you where you have to take it. It's near Connaught Place.'

Outside in the street, Richard bargained fiercely with an auto-rickshaw driver. He feels it's a point of honour not to be cheated. I feel I'd rather avoid unpleasantness. Having bargained until a fair price was agreed, we drove to the Central Court. The streets are wide in this part of town, with occasionally quite smart side roads and low expensive-looking dwellings. There are many trees and dusty pavements. The sights that remind you sharply that you are not in Europe might be the occasional cow standing around; a man in a loin cloth carrying a bundle on his head; a family of four on one lambretta; a man sitting on his heels brushing a lawn; a man slowly painting a wall in such a way that you cannot tell the bit he's painted from the crumbly bit he's coming to; a tiny child perhaps a year old sitting alone right by the busy road under a minute makeshift tent; a human just lying on the ground flat out and motionless; various strange garments of course and lovely saris. These memories flash through my mind. There are dozens more that I don't immediately recall, some quite shocking such as the sudden glimpse of a settlement of ragged tents on a bit of rough ground, with incredibly poor people sitting around.

'What on earth do these people do?' I asked Richard. 'What do they live on?'

'They're the affluent ones,' he replied. 'They've got a tent.' He laughed mirthlessly.

At the Central Court we ordered fresh lime juice and soda. It was marvellous. We chatted about the *Telegraph* and mutual friends while we waited for Serena and another girl called Jane to join us. They reminded me so much of two girls in a story by Ruth Jhabvala, I could hardly believe it. Perhaps it was just that they were two middle-class English girls in India and any two would have made me think of Ruth Jhabvala's *A Star and Two Girls*.

At one stage we realised, cursing, that we'd had ice with our drinks. The thought of what sort of water the ice was made from was pretty frightening. Serena said she'd accepted a drink on a camel farm recently and only after she'd knocked it back did it occur to her to ask where it came from. 'It's from our own open well,' she'd been told proudly and she had nearly fainted, but she'd come to no harm so she wasn't going to be scared now by a bit of ice.

Jane on the other hand had spent three days vomiting in agony after a meal in the most luxurious hotel in Udaipur. She now goes out of her way to eat risky things, to even it up I suppose. She ordered a salad for lunch, for example, washed in water from God knows where. The rest of us had very good curries and rice.

After lunch we separated, Jane to watch some golf champions practising for the Asian Games, and Richard and Serena to go shopping; and I went grimly back to Baroda House. Halfway there the driver of my auto-rickshaw inexplicably slowed to a halt.

'You want to get out?' he said, in an unfriendly way.

'Why—where are we?' I said.

'Here! Yes you go?'

'What are you talking about? I want to go to Baroda House for railway tickets.'

He grimaced wearily. I might have been saying Darjeeling Central Park, but he drove on. When he stopped again we were still not at Baroda House, or if we were, it had changed a lot since this morning.

'Baroda House,' he said rudely, so I got out and paid him. It turned out it was the other side of Baroda House. I found the Tourist Office again and saw at once that my man was there, so I joined the queue to see him. At the moment that my turn came another official arrived and they began a long conversation. As far as I could gather as a result of this conversation many things had to be written down in a large ledger. Sheaves of dollar notes were taken out and each note's number was entered in the great book. When a page was turned it involved a complicated process of rearranging sheets of carbon paper as well, because copies of everything were being kept. The man's handwriting was a hurried scrawl. It seemed inconceivable that anyone would ever want to check these millions of entries. I remembered a friend murmuring to me, 'If you ever need to reserve a rail seat ticket, take a book.'

I began to draw the scene but the second official noticed and told the first in Hindi; they both smiled and commented on what I was up to but seemed embarrassed, so I stopped. When he turned his attention to me the man explained that he could issue an Indrail Pass valid for fifteen days at a cost of fifty-eight pounds. It had to be paid in sterling. But the man who sent the telegrams to make the bookings was ill and, therefore, that couldn't be done. However, he might be back tomorrow in which case he would try to do them. It was interesting. This tired, friendly official who was bored and yet also responsible and even efficient at the nightmare task he had to perform was like the agent of an evil force bent on preventing one from moving by shattering one's will. Once he had spoken and defined the limits of my success nothing much seemed to make any difference. No bookings. He advised me to find the station master at each station as I arrived to check my booking.

Finally, he gave me two lots of paper saying these bookings could be arranged in Delhi. I must take them to the Central Reservation Office, Connaught Place. Each of these reservations must be made at a different queue. To save time he suggested finding the Chief Reservation Supervisor who could do both for me. 'Explain to him you cannot queue twice.'

I returned to the Central Court Hotel and, with Richard leading the way, walked with Serena to the Reservation Office. The approach to the low building was quite grand. A private road led through trees with various buildings and houses each side. It looked as if the railway personnel had almost their own compound, and this was it. All round there was a curiously indefinable sense of disorder. Unfinished repair work, some leaves swept into a heap but not removed, broken palings in the fence maybe, or a bit of machinery waiting aimlessly with wood piled against it . . .

The booking hall itself was like a horror scene from a film about the future. It was large and old-fashioned and empty of all furniture. It looked as if it had been in continual chaotic use since about 1914. Down one long side ran a series of numbered windows with lots of signs and writing describing why one should try one window rather than another. At each window there was a long impatient seething queue. Each queue twisted and moved like a snake. Individuals as yet unattached to a queue milled about looking agonised and holding great wads of papers. Serena took one look at it and said, 'I'll meet you outside—I'm going to write postcards.'

'How the hell do you find the supervisor?' I asked one or two men who looked as if they might know what they were doing but they passed by me like zombies, unaware in that madhouse that they had been spoken to.

'Ask at Enquiries,' said Richard, a most sensible and obvious thought that had not occurred to me. I was panicking a bit.

There was, of course just as long a queue at Enquiries, larger if anything. I went to the top of the queue and shouted, 'Where is the Chief Reservation Supervisor?' Through the general din someone heard and I seemed to hear his reply, 'Window One.' If the rest of the queue at Enquiries minded my behaviour they didn't show it. At Window One I could not face the queue but

Central Reservation Office, Connaught Place, Delhi

saw a door to the right. I went in. I was, as it were, backstage and here too a giant crowd moved and bustled about, obviously not much more ordered than the one out front. I found the Supervisor's desk. He was surrounded by petitioners already. I pushed through and sat down. Actually I didn't really push; somehow all the people standing around melted away if you looked as though you knew where you were heading.

The Supervisor, a grim fairly heavily-built man, looked at me challengingly. I explained what I wanted.

'I can do this one,' he said, 'this one you must take elsewhere.'

'I was informed most clearly that you could do both,' I said. 'That is why I have come to you.'

He actually rested his forehead on his hand for a moment inclining his head patiently. He looked me full in the eye. 'You were misinformed,' he said.

'I don't think so,' I persisted, feeling much more desperate than I hope I sounded.

'I will do this one,' he said with great finality. And he went away.

Central Reservation Office

The crowd had been watching all this with interest. I took out my drawing book and began drawing some of the girls dealing with the queue at Number One behind which I was now sitting. Several people came to look over my shoulder. Soon the Supervisor came back with one booking. 'Now you must take this one upstairs,' he said. I realised there were more levels of this extraordinary place. 'But first,' he continued grandly with a little smile, 'you must draw my photograph.'

'O.K.,' I said, 'then will you do the second booking?'

He acknowledged that I had spoken. I quickly drew a simple caricature of him. Muffled giggles from some of the girls and whispered comments came from behind my shoulder. Out of his mouth I drew a bubble. It said 'You have come to the wrong place, *but* I will help you!'

I gave it to him. First he pulled a little face, cocking his head on one side; then he smiled broadly and laughed. A girl called to him, 'Now you'll have to do it!' and laughed loudly. Very good-naturedly he got up, leaving the drawing on his desk, and went away.

By now the whole atmosphere had changed. I was surrounded by the most delightful crowd of smiling, laughing, helpful people. They asked where I came from, and who I worked for, and they described their visits to England. One lady said she had stayed in Cambridge. 'Why did you go to Cambridge?' I asked. 'It's nice there,' she said. 'London is too crowded.' I couldn't tell from her smile whether she was joking or not. The difference once they were on your side was amazing. A certain stony reserve quite vanished. People patted my arm, asked for my London address. 'If I pass through next year, I will visit you.' 'Please do.' They laughed and smiled and joked constantly.

The Supervisor returned with my bookings and I bid them all an affectionate farewell. I would have liked to stay longer. I may go back and do some more drawing.

Outside, Richard waited in the crowd. I told him what had happened. 'You're learning fast,' he said. It was as if he thought I had tricked them all, pulled a fast one on them. Serena was sitting on a kerbstone writing. We bargained with an auto-rickshaw for a ride to the Red Fort.

Up towards the Old Town the streets got progressively more crowded and more obviously run down and poor. Bicycle-rickshaws were common; you almost never see them in the centre of New Delhi. We passed several shanty town areas—more tent than shanty. The people looked at rock-bottom poverty level but there was considerable activity. Many individuals squatted on their heels, arms on their knees, resting or waiting; some lay stretched out as if quite unconscious or dead, but an equal number were busy cooking, talking, doing things.

The Red Fort is tremendously impressive. Very large, very

businesslike, with great sprawling grace and beauty. We were accosted almost at once by two beggar children. A quite pretty girl of about fourteen, very thin with huge, horribly sad eyes. The other was a boy. He had a stump instead of a right arm. He waved his stump in our faces and kept up a low-pitched monotonous whine that instantly infuriated me. I felt ridiculously angry with him. I gave the girl a two-rupee note I had in my pocket. I could sense, or thought I could, that Serena and Richard thought I was mad. The boy walked just in front of me, just slower than I was going so that I had continually to step round him. He droned on. I felt almost ready to give him something to shut him up but my mad hatred for him stopped me. He was too good at begging. It was all so practised it had lost its powers. The silent girl in black was easier to give to. Somehow she had left the decision to me.

Inside the Red Fort's Lahore Gate a man was selling catapults that launched little figures high in the air which then floated to earth on plastic parachutes. An enchanting little boy of about six ran to fetch the fallen toys. I bought several as stocking presents. While I fumbled for money the little boy smiled and looked enormously pleased and every now and then said 'Yes. Yes!' I smiled back at him and touched his little button nose and said 'Yes.'

It was calm and lovely inside the fort. Great Victorian barracks reared up flinty and British along one part of the interior park. The Indian army occupies them now, I think. In one little white marble open-air temple I paused and looked up at the sky. The afternoon light was fading and the white marble was silhouetted against the pink and yellow-streaked sky. Outside parrots squawked in the trees; near me some Indians walked silently, peering at the delicate inlaid wall decorations. I had the strong sensation that I had somehow become part of an illustration in a child's book. Everything became very unreal. It was by no means a pleasant experience and it left me feeling disturbed in the way a bad dream can. I was puzzled by this experience. I am writing this account of it the next day and the sensation has not completely left me.

As we left the fort we bought toys and odds and ends, glass necklaces, a small black marble pestle and mortar, a soap-stone figure of Ganesh brightly painted, and so on. Then we strolled over to Chandi Chowk, the wide, unbelievably congested shopping street that leads directly away from the fort.

'The only place in Delhi where you can get mugged,' said Richard, not very cheerfully.

I did not feel completely at ease here. It was so crowded and I was carrying so much, money and passports and tickets and the toys and odds and ends, and I was tired. But, in spite of that and Serena saying, 'I don't like this,' it was not something I would have missed. It is a great roaring bazaar with hooting scooter-taxis, carts, bicycles, rickshaws, pedlars, tourists, beggars, stallowners, crumbling buildings, water pumps and noise. The whole scene was lit last night with Diwali fairy lights, like Regent Street at Christmas time, gone raving mad.

We hailed a scooter and returned to the town centre to eat. Then I said goodbye to Richard and Serena who leave tonight for Simla.

Back at the hotel I wrote my journal for an hour or two and went to bed. But I was suddenly overcome with a dreadful feeling of anxiety. I felt restless and exhausted; dreadfully unhappy and alone; overwhelmed by the length of time that must pass before I'd be home and by the impossibility of ever catching these trains and finding these hotels that lay between me and my family. I tried to be reasonable and calm. I told myself I was tired, over-stimulated, trying to do too much, not allowing for the shock of India and its devastating effect on all my Western sensibilities. I wondered whether to ring my wife but was afraid that might make me feel worse and worry her. I tried to think that this awful feeling was all part of the dramatic experience of seeing India and must be felt and scrutinised just as much as anything else that might come my way. I wondered if I had caught an infection. I could feel my heart beating hard and sweat on my upper lip.

In the end I took a sleeping pill and read an essay by Isaiah

Berlin whose clear and elegant prose had some calming effect on my agitated mind.

I determined to take it easy next day.

Thursday 18th November

I had asked for an early morning call this morning and it awoke me from a deep but somehow not refreshing sleep. I had, as it were, a hangover from the disturbed feelings of yesterday night. Washing, shaving, and dressing in clean clothes, usually such powerful forces in setting me up for the day, did not work either. I felt angry with myself. I had an appointment at 10.00 with Arun Shourie, a distinguished journalist, at his house and I had woken early in order to write up this journal before I went. For the next couple of hours I drank coffee and wrote in the buffet, sometimes dreamily watching the waitress and waiters skilfully and politely serving the Japanese athletes, time keepers and coaches (all here for the Asian Games that open tomorrow) and the occasional Lunchtime O'Booze English sports writers or their Dutch or German colleagues. I wouldn't want to make too big a thing of it but it was impossible not to compare the heavy, pink, Europeans unfavourably with the

Buffet, Oberoi Hotel, Delhi

brown, neat and graceful Indians. The Japanese have their own special kind of awfulness. They are aggressively clean and shining, and seem to be dressed entirely in easy-wype-plastic-all-purpose-drip-dry-brite-material, and as each one has about a million-pounds worth of camera equipment round his neck and is sporting numerous badges that might be push buttons, they look like useful little gadgets on legs. I expect the ones I was observing are very, very good at throwing things and jumping along the ground. They are not nearly as polite to strangers as they might be, barely noticing other people on stairways and never allowing anyone to leave a lift first, although they are forever bowing to each other.

Anyway, I wrote and watched until it was time to go to see Arun. Each sortie I have made from my very grand hotel so far has been straight into up-town Delhi with everything that that means. Today my taxi turned down different ways and the route led through wide clean streets with fairly expensive-looking houses with little gardens, all dusty in the hot sunshine but without the bustle of the centre of town. But, here too in these comfortable suburbs, the same skinny cyclists went to and fro and individuals in dirty ragged clothes carried their mysterious burdens endlessly up and down. On the edge of a roundabout, a man might be sitting on the grass staring fixedly forward as if frantically trying to remember something, quite motionless and silent. I saw a gang of ragged men painting a zebra crossing. One held the paint pot, one wielded the brush, another held a piece of string taut to give a straight edge to the brush-man. Others manned a pushcart piled with battered equipment, and some squatted and watched patiently; all moved, if they moved at all, with majestic slowness. It sounds silly, but it was a beautiful sight: the beauty lay in the thin brown bodies and their slow deliberate movements and perhaps in the fact that behind these dirty, tattered comrades, lay a blinding white, extremely neat, brand-new, hand-painted zebra crossing.

I saw a man in white, wheeling a cart on which lay sprawled in the most abandoned posture, legs and arms flung wide, another man also in white. I saw a building site overgrown and rough with a little skirt of encroaching tents and shacks; in the centre was a lop-sided sign which read 'Site for Egyptian Embassy'. Bus shelters always seem to have a few people waiting in or near them. When a bus comes it doesn't exactly stop. It just swerves about a bit more than usual and like S.A.S. men on a mission-impossible, the waiting people start running. Suicidally dodging the other traffic that honks and peeps in exasperation they close on the bus which is by now accelerating away, except that it is so old and heavy it can't accelerate. Tubby old ladies, sandals slapping, saris awry, pelt down the road, outstripped by fleet young men and galloping gents, and as the bus finally grinds away and you expect there to have been the most horrible series of violent deaths you see, to your amazement, nothing. The passengers are all aboard, although 'aboard' doesn't quite convey the picture of the people clinging like mountaineers to the sheer walls of the outside of the bus.

The street life is wonderful. I simply cannot begin to imagine what it must be like to live like that, but for all its awfulness and hardship (or perhaps I should say, as well as its awfulness and hardship) there is something attractive about it. Not because it is quaint; perhaps it has a heroic quality. The people may be down but they are bloody well not beaten. They seem to say 'I'm going to catch that bus even though it doesn't stop,' and one respects and admires their resolve.

I thought of a speech that I cannot quote from memory, from Beaumarchais' *The Marriage of Figaro*, in which Figaro in a soliloquy pits himself against the Count, asking how the Count can possibly overcome him, Figaro? After all, in order to survive at all, let alone rise to his present position, he has had to fight and scheme and outwit and vanquish every second of every minute of his whole life. He is a veteran of countless battles, he only knows how to win, because if he doesn't win he's done for—that anyway is the gist of the speech and one responds to it with passionate approval. He deserves to win and you are certain he will. Some such feelings are evoked in me by the Indians I see in the streets. I do not exactly admire them, nor do I feel contemptuous of them; neither do I like or dislike them; but the healthy respect I have for their doggedness, or perseverance, or endurance, produces in me a feeling that somehow or other in the end they, like Figaro, will win.

Arun Shourie's house is a fairly new building. His father built it in a quiet shady back street and it is set in a little garden. A young man who was cleaning the windows came and pressed the door bell for me and yet another young man opened the door. I was shown into a cool comfortable sitting room. There were large modern oil paintings on the walls and the far wall was lined with books. The windows looked out onto the garden where a little grey squirrel ran hesitatingly along a washing line.

In a moment Arun Shourie came in. Every now and then you are lucky enough to meet someone with perfect manners. Perfect manners are an art and a skill on a level at least with the best cooking or clothes design or interior decorating. All are life-enhancing skills, but manners obviously have a personal quality missing in the others I've mentioned. To be made to feel welcome, and comfortable, at ease and interesting is a rare and intoxicating pleasure. Arun Shourie, whose courage during the emergency is well known, has in the last few days been through and is still going through a very serious professional crisis. In fact, for complicated political reasons, he's been fired from the editorship of *The Express*. So I felt extremely nervous of butting in on his life and therefore doubly grateful to him for not making me feel awkward.

We chatted about mutual friends and about his situation. He introduced me to his equally charming father who is now retired, and seems to spend his time painting. He showed me some of his latest work. They were huge oil paintings of water lilies on deep purplish-blue lakes. 'I can see who you've been looking at,' I said.

'I've had a full, interesting and rewarding life,' he replied. 'Now all I want to do is paint, like Monet.'

I haven't quoted him exactly: he meant he wanted to study Monet's technique and style and attempt to acquire some of his skill. One picture was a startling copy of a German Expressionist, startling because the brilliant colours clashed so violently with the delicate pinks and pale yellows and blues of the water lilies.

In Arun's sitting room I felt my nervous tension leaving me. The whole visit to his house had a calming and reassuring effect on me. I wished I could have stayed longer.

I told him I would like to see his friend Romesh Thapar, but that I'd had trouble getting hold of him, and that I'd be grateful if he could put me in touch with any artists or perhaps an art school.

He had a kind of portable telephone that he held in his hand. He explained he had so many phone calls starting at 6.00 in the morning that he'd bought this thing in Hong Kong to save time running up and down stairs.

A few calls later, several visits had been arranged, and shortly afterwards I left by taxi to see Thapar, the editor of the weekly journal *Seminar*.

His office is on Janpath and Connaught Place—back in the busy hot centre. Arun had given me very clear directions but the whole of the massive double-ringed Connaught Place is a jumble of very similar signs and buildings and when I found the doorway it was so dark and tiny, I began to doubt this could be the place. Several people were going in and out of the dark twisting staircase. I asked if this was where I'd find the *Seminar* offices. Some shrugged, some ignored me—getting on with doggedly surviving, I suppose—but one said 'Yes, *Seminar*,' so I went up and found my way to Romesh's office. His charm and manners were quite equal to Arun's, but Romesh is an older, more heavily-built man who gave me a different sort of welcome to that of the slender, exhausted, excessively quietly-spoken Arun. With Romesh I felt instantly completely at ease. I felt we understood each other and, in as much as it was possible, shared a view of the world.

I began talking too much and too fast, unburdening myself of my impressions and reactions. He listened, agreeing and laughing, got me a cool drink, and began talking himself.

'Of course,' he said. 'India knocks a Westerner sideways when he first arrives; all that noise, the huge crowds, the poverty and so on . . . but when we arrive in the West for the first time, we are shocked by all that rush. Why do they work so hard we wonder, what for? Get up at six, do this at half past, that at quarter to and on and on, rush here, rush there. What does all that rushing do? It saves you half an hour over the whole day, but what have you actually been doing? Westerners don't look any more, they do not see visually, they are trained to analyse.' In the context in which he was talking, which I cannot repeat verbatim, I took him to mean that there is a contemplative side to life that the West does not value enough; and he also meant that people should literally look inquisitively at what is actually going on around them, as Indians do.

As for the poverty here, he went on, 'It is dreadful, and it is a disgrace that more has not been achieved to alleviate it. But Indian poverty is not the same as Western poverty.' He hesitated, obviously wishing to make himself understood. 'There is a smile in Indian poverty,' he said. 'You see, it's kismet. They will always say kismet—fate—I have brought my suffering on myself. Fate has made me what I am and I am in control of my future.'

'Hang on,' I said, 'go back to "the smile in Indian poverty".' It was an expression that grated on me somewhat, and I think he sensed it. He smiled as if to say that it puzzles him almost as much as it obviously puzzles me; indeed later he more or less said so in so many words.

'I don't want to romanticise it,' he began, waving his hand, 'I know how awful, degrading, disgusting, poverty is.' He clearly needed no lectures from a Westerner about that. 'What I mean can only be understood in terms of the Hindu idea of the individual family. Sons look after their aged parents and even grandparents. The family is bonded together, bound to support each other and by extension they will also stand by those who are poor or worse off than themselves. Look, and you will see it is often not the rich who drop coins into the begging bowls, it is people almost as poor themselves. This creates a very special sort of poverty.' He went off at a tangent and began talking about something I'd already noticed. 'Everything in India is used. Nothing is thrown away. In Europe an old box or piece of broken machinery may be discarded; here it is made into firewood, fashioned into a toy, cannibalised for a spare part and put to a new use. People are busy, the old crafts are alive. The reason people are so interested in your drawing is because they value creativity very highly. We are an artistic and a creative people.'

I remembered, but didn't mention, seeing a television programme years ago during some prolonged power cuts. The television men were questioning people in the street about how they'd cope when all the lights went out that evening. 'I don't know—it's totally disgusting—when you think of the old people and the kiddies—the government has brought this on itself—something should be done. What can we do, we are helpless . . .' the English moaned and wailed.

At last the interviewer found an Indian. 'Excuse me, sir,' he said with that ever so slightly exaggerated politeness that is meant to signal complete unawareness of the man's colour. 'What will you do when the power goes off tonight?'

The man looked slightly puzzled.

'How will you cook your supper? How will you do it in the dark?'

'I will light a lamp,' said the Indian, still not understanding what the idiot with the microphone was on about.

'Oh, you've taken precautions and laid in a lamp have you?'

'I'll make a lamp.'

The interviewer expressed incredulous surprise. '*Make a lamp!*' he cried. 'How will you make a lamp?'

'I will make the lamp out of ghee—and if necessary I'll cook on it as well. Good evening,' said the Indian.

It had struck me at the time that that man had certain qualities and knowledge and skills that made the television man festooned with electronic equipment look ridiculous. The Indian was a poorer, and perhaps a less educated man, but a better survivor.

Romesh continued, 'A few years ago my wife and I were in New York and we were taken around the most run-down areas of that city. Queens, Brooklyn, Harlem,' he paused, 'and we were horrified, it was devastating, it was an appalling experience. We had never before seen the deep melancholy of Western poverty. By our standards the people were well off. They had clothes, cars, radios and so on, but they were so melancholy, so utterly sad.' It had obviously been a terrible shock for him.

He talked about China, another country he had visited. 'There you see no poverty really. They are another creative close-knit people. But they (he meant now the Communists) have damaged their country. They have destroyed the old arts and crafts. Every exhibition tells the same gigantic lie that nothing of worth happened in China before the revolution. But both China and India, in their different ways, have created wealth. People don't notice that but it is important and true. Both can be independent of the rest of the world.' He also said that the Chinese had paid too horrifying a price in blood for the benefits their revolution has brought them. 'Nothing is worth that.'

His wife, who had joined us, spoke. 'They asked the wrong question. Once you ask "Freedom or Bread?" you are lost. You must have both,' she said firmly.

'Things are changing here,' said Romesh. 'The gap between the very rich, living corruptly on the black economy, and the very poor, is becoming too wide and that means trouble. The lowest caste, the Untouchables, are rising. They want to claim their rights. They want a share in the wealth they have helped create. They are no longer passive. There is a new attitude, for instance, to rape. Hitherto a man from a high caste could simply take a good-looking low-caste woman and use her. She would not resist. She would be afraid. Now both she and her menfolk will resist. They bring charges of rape. It is a new crime. The low castes are even converting to Islam sometimes to assert their individuality.'

'Incidentally, Mrs Gandhi's success lies partly in her skill at bringing together the Hindu and the Muslim community. Anyone who can combine their support can make a government.'

We talked a little about Communism and the curious fact that there are idealistic Communists who wouldn't personally hurt anyone and yet remain loyal to the most bloodthirsty and cruel political gangsters around. They can and do turn a blind eye to the frightful crimes of the party and can busy themselves trying to set up a state of affairs in which these crimes will most certainly be committed again.

This conversation was held in Romesh's quiet office with a fan turning slowly above our heads. Outside, Connaught Place roared and honked. Now and then a man came in with a note for Romesh. Sometimes he and his wife discussed whether or not to take a trip to Rajasthan. Several times I made to go, loathe to break off the conversation but anxious not to wreck Romesh's morning's work. He waved me back to my seat. 'No, no, no,' he said, 'I am doing my work while we are talking.'

Once when Romesh left the office for a moment he said to his wife, 'Explain to Nicholas the smile in Indian poverty.' I fancied his wife didn't exactly warm to this task. For a moment she appeared not to understand what Romesh had said and he repeated his request. There was silence for a minute after he had gone. Then she said, 'We were in New York and were shown the poor run-down areas, Brooklyn, the Bronx . . . it was terrible, terrible. It was worse, that's all, worse than Indian poverty.' Even the memory seemed to stir up the horror of these places.

Probably it's silly to make such comparisons. After a certain point perhaps poverty is just poverty, in the same way that there is very little difference between having five million pounds and a hundred million. The other element which makes comparisons nonsensical is the weather.

Romesh said, 'You see we have our summer. For six months it goes on and on and on. You think it's hot now,' he glanced out at the hot morning sun, 'but it's not, it's cold now. In the summer you can't move. You've got to slow down or stop. This obviously makes a difference. In Delhi and most of India you can sleep anywhere most of the time without freezing to death or dying of exposure . . . I don't know . . .'

In case I have conveyed the wrong impression, Romesh and his wife are appalled by the poverty in India and nothing they said diluted their straightforward abomination of it, or went any way to excuse or deny it.

Again I was very sorry to leave but knew I must go. I had told them I would like to meet some artists and they immediately tried to ring Krishna Khanna, whom Arun had also tried unsuccessfully to call; and they gave me a letter of introduction to the director of a nearby arts centre, where there is an art school, drama school and gallery.

Before I left Romesh I asked if I could go to the lavatory. 'Oh yes, of course,' he said, calling a servant to direct me. The man fumbled for a key and bowed slightly to indicate that I should follow him. 'I hope there is some water,' said Thapar in a worried voice. 'The lavatory is perfectly all right, I just hope there is some water; if there isn't, never mind,' he finished cheerfully.

I followed the servant down a corridor and he stopped at a door. He unlocked it and inside was a large, clean room of bare grey cement. It gave the impression of grey cleanliness. There was simply a wash basin on one wall and a lavatory nearby. When I had used the lavatory I pulled the chain. No water.

It was a typical little incident, that illustrated the complicated contradictions of India. Romesh Thapar is famous all over India. He is enormously respected and admired and widely read. He is cultured, wise and well-travelled (all this is for Westerners who may not have heard of him; I'm aware that it is the equivalent of an Indian taking time out to identify, say, Isaiah Berlin) but in spite of all this, and his comfortable airy bookish office, and having a servant to lead his visitors to the lavatory, the lavatory has no water in it.

Regretfully I left the Thapars. They had arranged to leave Delhi tomorrow morning but they said if they change their plans they'd call me and we'd have dinner.

I took an auto-scooter to the arts centre. The director was out. I was quite glad as Mrs Thapar had said, 'Don't let her talk you into the ground.' I explained to a lady I met in the corridor that I was interested in seeing the art school; she said that although it was closed in the afternoon I was welcome to go up and look around.

There were a number of studio rooms off a corridor and all had one or two students in them. They were sitting around reading, chatting; one was sifting through some photographs.

I didn't like to barge in but on the other hand if I didn't, I wouldn't see any paintings. I went into a room and introduced myself to the very young, very shy, first year student who was there. She looked at me amazed as I explained I'd like to see her painting and talk to her for a moment. But she was very polite, answered my questions monosyllabically and showed me a huge painting she was doing of some mushrooms. I asked if she had done it from life. 'No, out of my head,' she replied.

I moved on to another room where a boy was looking through photographs. He too nearly died of embarrassment and could not really answer my questions. He too was a beginner. 'Please look around quite freely,' he said with a sweet smile.

I tried a third room. This looked both more promising and more daunting. Two ladies, one perhaps thirty, one considerably older, were painting. Each worked at quite a hefty canvas. They took no notice of me. I approached and explained I'd like to ask them some questions. They were less shy than their young colleagues and more ready to talk. I tried my questions again.

'I notice that all the paintings in this school are abstract paintings. Could you tell me what is the influence that has pointed you all in this direction? Is it perhaps from a Western school of painting?'

'What do you mean, abstract?' said the young woman, standing boldly in front of her splotchy picture.

'I mean not representing anything from the material world,' I said, stung by her challenging reply. 'I have not seen any representational pictures.'

'What do you mean, representational?' she countered, carefully wiping a brush.

'Some pictures one sees are of trees,' I said, 'and fields, or of still-life arrangements in which you can identify flowers or plates or other familiar objects.' She seemed to be very mildly irritated and at the same time puzzled.

The older woman looked around. 'He's quite right,' she said.

The younger woman said, 'When we start here we study from life, that is for beginners, we practise our skill at drawing in order later to be able to express our inner feelings.' She went on to say that the only influence she was aware of was that of the famous and successful artist who ran the place.

She then apparently lost interest in the conversation and left the room. I chatted to the older, rather more friendly woman, who said she'd been a student here for eight years.

After a bit the first lady returned with a much younger girl dressed in European clothes, who said 'Can I help you? Please sit down.' She led me to a chair.

In answer to my question she said, 'All the aesthetic qualities that are found in abstract painting, interest in pure form, colour and composition are, of course, basic in all traditional forms in Indian art and always have been. When certain artists in Europe discovered these qualities and began to produce abstract paintings naturally we responded to them.'

'So, you do not consider abstract painting a Western invention?'

'Not at all.'

She was superbly confident, cool and polite and unfriendly. We did not take the conversation very far. She knew a certain amount about European art and quite liked some of it, but that was about it. She was very solemn and never smiled, except politely when I said goodbye.

I thought the paintings were dreadful. The worst kind of second-rate abstract nonsense: meaningless incoherent forms that were only very vaguely recognisable as human or vegetable. The large picture of mushrooms was about the nearest thing to a thought-out work I saw, but it was much too big. The size of a painting is extremely important. A painting does not get more interesting by simply getting bigger; often the contrary is true.

Earlier in the day Romesh, Arun and Arun's father had all tried to call Krishna Khanna, the famous painter, to arrange for me to visit him and perhaps go with him to see a painters' colony near his house. The phone system had failed them all. I also tried and failed after I returned to the Oberoi but as Romesh had given me Krishna Khanna's address and urged me to call on him, I took a taxi to his address. His house was in an estate which is built on a grid system which I imagine is a fairly common style here. Once inside the system, there is a signpost at every intersection telling you which numbers lie in which direction. The roads are rough with grassy edges and trees shade the way. The houses lie back from the road in somewhat ragged gardens. The usual mysterious pedestrians pace patiently towards their destinations or rest immobile by the roadside. Some seek the cool shade of a tree, some seem to have sat down on their heels just where they were when their springs unwound. I haven't yet seen a man or woman in the act of sitting down or standing up. They are always either walking or squatting.

We found what I thought must be the address. I approached the house and saw a sign which said it was a school. I thought 'Blast!' A woman with one arm in plaster was just opening the gate to an elderly woman who was making heavy weather of the walk from the roadside.

'Excuse me,' I said. 'I am looking for the residence of Mr Khanna and I'm not sure . . .'

'This is the residence of Mr Khanna,' said the younger of the two women. Her tone was sharp, suspicious and obviously intended to give the impression that she was not going to stand any nonsense from me. This brisk attitude seems to me more common in women than men here. All the men I have met have been extremely courteous, if somewhat reserved on first meeting. Sometimes in asking directions in the street, I have delighted quite as much in the beautiful manners of the strangers I have accosted as I have in receiving their help. But the women, such as those in the art school, can be quite frosty at first although they may warm up a little later. I wonder if this is generally true or whether I've just imagined it. Perhaps it's because I look rather bad tempered; people say that about me sometimes when I've been in the best of spirits. It can be quite irritating; I can find myself snapping 'Rubbish, I'm not feeling at all bad tempered . . .' And of course they feel justified.

I explained to Mrs Khanna, whom she turned out to be, that I was a friend of Arun's, but this seemed not to impress her one bit. 'Mr Khanna is away,' she said. 'In Simla as a matter of fact.' I do not mean to say she was rude, but she was walking a fine line between politeness and downright coolness.

'Then please excuse me for disturbing you,' I said, beginning to walk away.

'Well, you may as well come in and see the pictures and have some tea,' she said, as if to say, 'Well don't just go away in a huff—good heavens!'

She told my taxi driver to wait. 'Will he mind?' I asked, all middle-class English anxiety. She looked at me almost disbelieving her ears. 'Why should he mind,' she said, waving her good arm. 'The meter's going. He's getting paid.' But the Sikh driver looked intensely annoyed.

Inside, the house was cool and comfortable. There were many paintings on the wall. I was very struck by one bright painting of two figures. It showed that Indian celebration when they squirt coloured water at each other. It was painted in the fifties by Hussein. There was another picture by him, a more recent one that was also very good. I tried to look at, and say the right things about Khanna's paintings, but for me Hussein's pictures were much more interesting and I kept going back to them. We sat and had tea, Mrs Khanna keeping up her tart manner. She offered me a little cookie, like a large, soft, round, dusty marble. 'Thank you,' I said, taking one. 'What is it?'

'Eat it and you'll find out,' she said. This was definitely not playing the game.

'What is your profession?' I asked, tired of hearing about Mr Khanna. To my amazement she seemed almost visibly to deflate.

'Oh,' she said, 'I'm a—I'm a teacher.'

'Oh!' I said nonplussed and wondering at the change.

'Also,' she said, rallying, 'a psychologist.'

'My wife is also a psychologist,' I said quickly. Knight to King four. 'A child psychologist and also a psychotherapist. She works at a large London Teaching Hospital.'

'She works with children?' said Mrs Khanna rather desperately.

'Her work as a child psychologist is for a London Borough—that is, of course, with children of all ages.'

I wouldn't swear to it but it seemed to me Mrs Khanna became more friendly at this point. That doesn't quite say what I mean. She was not being unfriendly before, she was being disconcerting. I felt that if I led with my chin she'd clock me, but after this we became more relaxed. Perhaps I was nervous and she was picking up my uncertainty.

'The little cakes are left over from Diwali,' she said. 'We eat them at Diwali—it's traditional.'

I was becoming aware that outside my taxi was honking impatiently. She walked me to the front gate and became downright charming and warm. 'You haven't left me your address,' she said. 'What a pity you missed my husband.'

'I will write to you and give you my address,' I said. 'And when you are next in London I hope you will visit us.'

'Thank you. I would like to. Do not forget to write.'

'I won't. Thank you for the tea. I hope I have not disturbed your day.'

Again a look of incredulity, 'Of course not. It was a pleasure to meet you. Goodbye.'

Back at the hotel I wrote Caroline a long letter sitting at a table under a sickle moon in the twilight. It grew dark as I wrote but someone eventually turned some lights on.

I didn't want to spend another evening alone and to my delight I saw a message in my pigeon hole. I hoped madly that it was an invitation but in fact it was from Romesh saying we couldn't dine together, but would I telephone.

I booked some hotels for my train journey that starts the day after tomorrow by going to the travel agency in the lobby, and tried and tried to get through to Romesh, but failed. Then I rang Mrs Prabha Dutt, a friend and colleague of Tandon, the *Daily Telegraph* stringer in Delhi. I had spoken to her on my first day and she'd said perhaps I'd like to come and have coffee one day. She was out at first but her husband said to call again, so I did. First she said she'd come to the hotel for coffee with her husband, then said perhaps I'd rather come to them. Shamelessly I said, 'Yes, please, I'd much rather.' So she extremely kindly asked me to eat with them. It turned out that the family was already eating when I telephoned so it was more than kind, it was terrific. She stopped eating and waited for her husband to come and get me in the car.

To sit and have a family supper with the room untidy and with pretty children running in and out was an enormous pleasure. I had never really understood quite what people passing through London meant when they said how much they'd enjoyed similar dinners with my family. Now I understood. The house was comfortable and the food was simple and delicious. I can't really remember much about the conversation except that it was funny and lively. I was very impressed with Prabha: she has a very quick mind and a somewhat abrasive personality but is affectionate and fond with her husband and children. She peeled me a tangerine.

'Here, you must have some salt on that,' said Mr Dutt, whose Christian name I never caught.

'Salt!' I cried. 'On a tangerine?'

'Yes,' he said. 'You've just been eating rice pudding. The tangerine will taste very sour without salt.'

'No thanks, I'll have it straight,' I said.

He looked doubtful. 'Look, it's no trouble at all, I've got salt right here—try it,' and he sprinkled salt on the bit in my hand.

It tasted awful, but he sprinkled salt all over the rest as well.

Later we went to their bedroom to watch a B.B.C. programme about the Indian Press. Prabha lay on her bed with her two daughters reading beside her. A servant came in for some money. Mr Dutt sat near me telling me who was who on the programme. It was very pleasant and friendly and later Mr Dutt drove me home.

Friday 19th November

The mood of anxiety and depression that had rather affected the last two days had lifted. I don't know why, or even what produced the disagreeable feeling in the first place. Its going had a great deal to do with having met Arun and Romesh. They displayed a side of India which, if it were lacking, would make India hell. It is highly intelligent, worldly and resolute. They are men made up of a certain mixture of courage, common sense and shrewdness with Indian courtesy, a sense of fairness, and patience delicately included. There is no doubt that they and others I met afterwards calmed and reassured me.

I spent the whole of the morning writing my journal because I wanted to get down as quickly as possible my recollections of the conversations with these men. It was not until nearly 1.00 that I took a taxi to the Saga Travel Agency to meet Narendra Taneja who had promised to introduce me to some cartoonists today. At the Saga office two of the young men I'd met before greeted me in a friendly way, but said Narendra was not here as he had had to leave town. I was disappointed but also knew this gave me an opportunity for some sightseeing that otherwise I would miss.

'He may be back later at one thirty,' said one of the boys. He left it open whether I waited or left and came back. I decided to go for a walk and come back, and if he had not returned by then, to go and see some tourist places.

Outside I hesitated, wanting to find my way back to the

Government Handcraft Emporium to buy some silk for Caroline. A smiling old Sikh came up to me. 'What are you looking for, sir?' he said.

'The Government Handcraft Emporium,' I said, studying my notes.

'Come with me,' he said in a paternal sort of way, 'I'll show you.'

I knew he was on the make, but was quite interested to see where he'd take me. He asked me what country I came from. Indians do not seem to hear the difference between the various accents in which English is spoken and cannot easily tell an American from a German or an Englishman.

He said he had been to Bradford, but a sort of breezy vagueness about when and what it was like made me wonder. We picked our way down various little alleys until I became fed up. I was going too far and was anyway almost certainly going to finish up at some little stall of his own. 'Where are we going?'

He pointed onward. 'We are nearly there,' he said, directing my gaze across a main road to another little side street crowded with wandering, sitting, milling Indians.

'Too far,' I said. 'Sorry.'

'No sir, no distance.'

'Considerable distance,' I said. I turned down the main road which led roughly back to my starting point. I heard him protesting behind me, but strolled on. I have taken to walking very slowly. It's partly the heat and partly to help slow down everything, including my feverish mind. It helps me to keep India at a distance. You don't run from it, you just let it wash over and past you. Similarly, when accosted by would-be salesmen or guides I pause, look at them for a moment, perhaps smile slightly and only then say, 'No thank you.' A hurried refusal will produce a quick argument in favour of the proposal: 'Very cheap, no obligation, only five rupees, just look,' and so on. Whereas silence tends to produce silence, slowness produces slowness and this, of course, gives you time to extricate yourself from the undesired encounter. I would like to emphasise I am not being rude when I behave like this; indeed it is hard to be rude to such well-mannered and courteous people, but it is interesting how well it works.

The old man was disappointed and hurt and angry. I saw him reflected in a shop window standing and wondering whether to follow me. His expression of pain hurt me. I did not want to disappoint him but he had asked for it. After all, he'd set it up, he'd taken a risk with me. I might have paid off. In order to ensnare me he had been excessively friendly and chatty and flattering ('Ah England. What a great people!') But it was not just friendliness, it was business. There was money in it and it's irritating the way Indian dealers try to make you feel guilty for not buying something while endlessly repeating, 'Just look, sir—no obligation.' They convey a lot of obligation. What they say with their eyes is, 'Do you actually want me to starve, to fail?' What they say in words is, 'But this is beautiful silk.' The voice then drops into a concerned lower tone: 'Don't you want to buy something good for madam?' The implication is you will be admitting to serious marital trouble if you don't buy a hideous shiny handbag. It can get wearing.

I went to a bookshop to look at art books. I particularly want to find a book on the Kalighat school of painting, but so far I cannot find anyone, artist or bookseller, who has ever heard of this profoundly beautiful and influential work.

The bookshop was well stocked and had a great many art books, but not what I was looking for, although I did find a pretty book on glass painting.

I did a drawing in the bookshop. It was quiet, cool and dimly lit and was like a bookshop should be. It had old wooden shelves smoothed and polished by years of browsers. Fans turned slowly on the ceiling and high up on the top of most shelves were piles of papers and books, probably put there decades ago and now collecting layer after layer of dust, and quite forgotten. The interiors of such Indian shops, the railway station offices here and the ticket offices at tourist spots, often remind me powerfully of Dickens. There is the same air of decaying tradition that Dickens celebrates in his descriptions of old shops

Oxford Book & Stationery Co., Delhi

and houses. Much time has passed and no one has cleaned up after it. Small broken implements have not been replaced or mended but are used just as they are. I saw a rubber stamp saying 'Paid' with a cracked handle and the pad almost worn away. It's almost like a working display of the past in a modern museum. Every detail of these places is smoothed, rounded, chipped and worn by use, and giving a kind of pleasure that a brand new, electronic, plastic-finished object cannot.

In this sense life in India is in many ways life in Victorian England, or even earlier, and I find that aspect enormously pleasing and delightful; particularly as it is possible to escape easily back into the thoroughly modern eighties any time you want to. For comfortably-off tourists it is, anyway.

Back at the Saga office, Narendra Taneja was sitting at his desk. He shook hands and I reminded him of his offer to introduce me to some cartoonists. He set about making phone calls and meanwhile ordered drinks from the stall nearby, fetched by one of his assistants.

Narendra is an impressive young man, ambitious and articulate and obviously with considerable initiative. Although he runs his travel agency he only spends a couple of hours a day there. The rest of the time he has other fish to fry. I didn't discover exactly what, but journalism plays a major part in it.

After a bit he said everything was fixed. He'd take me over to the *Times* building, which housed several newspapers, and introduce me to a distinguished writer who'd show me round. Then he said, 'Come back to my office at five and we'll talk.' I explained I had to return to my hotel sometime before meeting some people at seven. 'No problem,' he said, 'I'll be here until five thirty. Then I'll show you how to get to your friends. What is their address?' I showed him the name and address and he whistled with surprise and respect. 'These are very important influential people,' he said. 'They live five minutes from here.'

Walking through the streets talking to Narendra was very different from walking alone. With him I merged more into the scene. No one accosted me except for a beggar woman. I happened to have some small coins in my pocket and gave them to her. She persisted in her demands and received a curt and pretty ferocious stream of Hindi from Narendra. I felt protected and more as if I belonged while in his company.

The visit to the newspaper offices was very confusing. For a start the building is very big and I never had the faintest idea where I was or which newspaper's rooms I was in. It can be difficult to tell an editor or a super-important writer from an office boy, because everyone wears open-necked shirts and various kinds of Indian clothes that I can't at once identify as being expensive or cheap. They spoke very quietly and when they were using Indian names, as they were doing all the time in the newspaper building, what I heard sounded something like this, 'We will just mumble, mumble, the next floor you can meet mumble, mumble of the mumble, mumble. He is quite important because he comes from mumble, mumble and therefore knows mumble,' and so on. I didn't know who anyone was although they were all, as usual, apparently pleased to meet me and good-naturedly stopped whatever they were doing and talked, or joined our tour.

The atmosphere of the newspaper office was very familiar to me. It was very like the *Telegraph*. People moved along the corridors, paused and chatted, called into other offices, and messengers lolled about.

After a bit I found myself sitting in the office of a cartoonist whose name I never caught but to whom I took an instant liking. He was about my age, slow and quiet of speech, and had the air of a man who might smile at any moment; some permanent, slight, private amusement was expressed in his eyes and mouth.

It turned out that the two top cartoonists I'd come to meet were at the opening of the Asian Games and I was sorry to miss them for they are very good political cartoonists. However, the one I did meet made up for my disappointment.

All of a sudden an extraordinary figure leapt into the room. Nijinsky's famous soaring entrance in *Le Spectre d'une Rose* had nothing on the chap. His appearance was as wild as his manner. Thick black hair stood out all over his head at least two feet long; now and again his face vanished completely behind it and he brushed it aside looking like a swimmer coming up for the second time. A week's growth of beard covered his cheeks and chin and he was thin as a rail. His clothes were in a vaguely hippy style.

'Hi man, it's really great to meet you. I was wondering whether we could do an interview, nothing too heavy at all, just maybe sit around. I'll just listen, maybe we could rap a little like about your scene and where everything is, like not necessarily everything, O.K., great? Yeah, I'm not interrupting, am I?' The strange young man grinned and frowned simultaneously, and always waited until someone else had started speaking before he began a question. He was deeply in love with the sixties when 'We didn't bomb anyone and were just—well it was to do with love and of course there was John Lennon . . .' He rambled on. The cartoonist gazed at him affectionately, smiling gently and waiting.

Another cartoonist came in, a silent man who spoke almost no English. I was told later he was one of the most widely-known cartoonists in the country and worked for a Hindi paper. He had brought some of his drawings to show me and they were very good.

The weird young man began to get even more restless. 'Perhaps we could get out,' he said, 'like continue to rap downstairs.'

'Where downstairs?' said the big calm cartoonist.

'Like the mezzanine.'

We went downstairs to a canteen and had some pretty awful coffee. Waving my arm to emphasise a point, I knocked over a full glass of water. It shattered with a loud crashing sound.

'Great!' yelped the young man. 'That's real! Oh yeah, that's really passionate.'

'That's extremely careless,' I said, annoyed with myself.

'Oh no, that's what should happen. I love the sound of smashing glass,' he said earnestly, almost yearningly. The cartoonist stood smiling, quietly amused at this completely absurd situation.

Conversation was meaningless. I could understand very little either of them said, but I liked the cartoonist enormously and now and then we managed to exchange a few words that were comprehended by both of us.

We went back upstairs. The cartoonists' room was now chock-a-block with a new crowd. They seemed to be part of a moving conference, because they all left at once. The interview continued.

'Like what do you think of England being a second-rate power now?' said the hairy, staring-eyed young man.

'I do not think about it,' I said. 'England is in fact pretty powerful and . . .'

'That's great; didn't you just love the sixties?'

'No, I'm terribly sorry, I hated them.'

His face really fell. 'But they were—I mean, we didn't bomb anyone. Everything was fine then, we really solved all the problems and loved everything.'

'If you solved all the problems, how come all the old problems are still with us?' I asked.

He looked appalled, and I could have kicked myself.

'They were great days, you know . . .'

Somehow my cold Western manner affected him badly, and I tried again. 'I know I'm sounding all tough and unsympathetic, but nothing was solved by flower power and love and the Beatles,' I said.

'We thought it was, it seemed as if it was,' he said lamely.

'Well, you were wrong, I'm afraid.'

'The world was different then.'

'Not really—*you* were different. The world hasn't changed that much.'

'It was so wonderful.'

'You were young.'

He couldn't bear it and soon he left the room mumbling goodbyes.

I felt terrible. I appealed to the cartoonist. 'I was trying to answer his questions, but I upset him.'

'Not at all, no, no, not a bit.'

'Yes, I did.'

'No, no, he will write something now, he is a very good journalist.'

'He's like a child—he's a nut-case.'

'No, no, he's very nice, he's a good journalist.'

Later Narendra sent me a cutting of the wildly-unlikely piece the young man wrote. Here it is with a portrait of me by the sleepy cartoonist.

A CARTOONIST CALLS ON WEEKEND

Well your boy was sitting nice and quiet, thought he was sitting looking *real* pretty too when WHAM in rushed the asst. editor, and your boy must be forgiven for thinking he was going to be done in for good or something. But exactly!

Hell he grabbed me by the lapels of my frayed Levi jacket, yanked me up—and the next thing your boy knew he was face to face with Nick Garland of London's *Daily Telegraph* if you please.

'Take him out for a coffee . . . or something'—those were your boy's orders. But this boy poor boy was plumb out of cash, see. So what do you think your boy did. He took two bucks from a fellow journalist and took him down to the mezzanine—for coffee of course. But exactly!

Now your boy's no Tom Wolfe not by a long shot sweetie so what's he to say?

To Nick Garland (put me in mind of Judy Garland, Gawd bust her hairy soul), who's the staff cartoonist for the *Telegraph*, 'political' as he insisted on punctuating afore the word 'cartoonist'.

Over black coffee (his suit was from Macy's, N.Y.) Garland thawed a leetle-teetle bit and gave out his parents had left England soon after the Blitz (World War II bombing of London) and so he was brought up amidst the sylvan surroundings of New Zealand.

At 19 years of age (he's 47 now) he returned to London and studied at the Royal School of Art. During the early '60s he worked with theatre people, rubbing tweeds with intergalactic figures like Arnold Wesker, Harold Pinter, John Lennon, Robert Bolt, Barry Bermange, Alan Sillitoe, Samuel Beckett . . . and a glittering galaxy of others.

WOW!!!

Soft-spoken, blue-eyed, mousy-thatched Garland later moved in with *Punch* and also worked for *Private Eye*.

Alas just when things were getting hot half *The Hindustan Times* burst in crowding ol' Nick with their arty-arty efforts. He broke a glass. At this your boy retreated with two thank-you's and the oouchhy memory of a rather powerfully firm handclasp.

G'bye ol' boy see you in Blighty, right g'bye g'bye . . . And zat was zat.

—ARUN SHUNGLOO
from *Weekend Review*,
a *Hindustan Times* publication
26 December 1982

He gave me a book of his cartoons. I thanked him and asked him to write in it. He wrote 'With love to Mr Garland' and signed his name, Sushil Kalra.

I left the newspaper building as baffled and confused as I have been since I arrived in India. I left messages for the two men I had hoped to meet, saying I was sorry to miss them. Lots of people shook hands and promised to come and see me at the *Telegraph* one day. I hope they do.

I returned to the hotel, wrote a bit, had a sandwich, and returned to Narendra's office. He ordered samosas and cold drinks from next door. They were brought in by a little raggedy boy.

Narendra's brother was there with a friend, both of them left-wing students; and his sister came in and sat in the back of the office.

While we chatted to Narendra against the noise of the busy street outside people came and went, quiet conversations were held, food was served. The office was porous: the street and life flowed through it. Narendra sat calmly, sometimes speaking into the phone, sometimes explaining some point to me. He described his brother's left-wing views and explained why they were wrong.

'Why doesn't he argue with you?' I said, catching the brother's eye. He sat, apparently quite unconcerned, listening to himself being described as mistaken.

'Oh, we've often argued,' said Narendra. His brother smiled broadly but said nothing.

Later when I again urged the younger man to speak, Narendra waved a beckoning arm. 'All right,' he said, 'you can join us.' The two young men were only sitting the other side of the desk, no further from Narendra than I was. They both acknowledged the invitation, but neither spoke. However, we were joined by another young man, who immediately began a long speech about Mrs Gandhi. He spoke earnestly, addressing himself to me as if I were a pupil. He said that Mrs Gandhi was not doing well, but on the whole, and for the time being anyway, he supported her. He thought, however, that the time would come when she would be swept away although at the moment there was no contender for her place and she made damn sure there wouldn't be.

(I remembered another critic of Mrs Gandhi who had gone as far as to say that Sanjay's death was for Mrs Gandhi a personal tragedy but a political gain.

'That is why she was able to survive it and go on. You see she wanted to create a dynasty so she brought Sanjay on. But he came on too fast. By the time he died he controlled too many politicians. He had become a threat. She didn't only lose a son, she lost a rival. I know,' went on this speaker, 'that this is a dreadful thing to say, but it's true. Now she is trying to bring on her second son, but that is hopeless, he moves too slowly.'

'Would Sanjay have been a dangerous man?'

'He already was a dangerous man. I cannot prove it but he was a murderer.' Others listening at the time agreed with the speaker and several said, 'Yes, he was certainly a murderer.')

The earnest young man went on to say that Mrs Gandhi ruled her party absolutely. Her word was law. No one dared cross her or question her decisions. He said it was not impossible that she quite welcomed things getting a bit out of hand—trouble with the Sikhs, independent movements here and there, general unrest, because if it got bad enough she would be able to bring back a state of emergency. (Others I spoke to later, when asked their opinion on this theory, said it was far-fetched.)

I asked him if he thought Mrs Gandhi was by nature a dictator, if she wanted absolute power.

'No,' he replied. 'She wants to do well for her people but the system does not work. The rich get richer, the poor mark time. She feels that only by the ruthless exertion of total power can the situation be improved. She would prefer the democratic way, she is a democrat but she is impatient and gets frustrated.' (In this he agreed with my other informants, who had described Mrs Gandhi as a natural-born dictator with a grand dose of acquired democracy in her make-up. She wants most of all to be a popular dictator, a dictator by acclaim.)

Narendra and the students listened to the young man without comment. I could not tell what they thought. Once or twice Narendra caught my eye as I looked enquiringly at him but he just smiled and let the other continue. I felt Narendra thought it would interest me to hear these views even if he didn't altogether agree with them.

The newcomer also talked about Arun Shourie. He obviously knew him and feared that Arun would now find it difficult to publish his views in any paper. Government pressure would prevent it.

'Would the government close the newspaper if it published such stuff?' He shook his head. 'No, no, we have a free press, it doesn't work like that. The newspapers are owned by very rich men. They own and run many big industries. They rely completely on government contracts and permits and if they step out of line in their newspapers their business elsewhere begins to suffer.'

Rather abruptly the young man stood up and he and the students said goodbye and left the room. Later when I was leaving I found they hadn't gone but were all sitting quietly downstairs. I asked Narendra who he was. It turned out he wasn't a student as I had first thought but a teacher. 'He is very nice,' said Narendra with a smile, somehow conveying to me that I shouldn't perhaps take it all too literally.

I asked Narendra which of our politicians were known in his country. 'Mr Callaghan,' he said promptly.

'Why him?'

'Because he is a good friend of India and a great trade-union leader.'

'Great trade-union leader?' I said. 'He was in the navy and has spent his life as a politician in the Labour Party.'

'Oh? We have learnt that he is a great trade-union leader.'

'O.K. Who else?'

'Mr Heath, he made a very good speech here recently and works hard for the third-world countries.'

'The Brandt Report?'

'Yes.'

'Anyone else?'

'Mrs Thatcher, of course, and Mr Foot. Mr Foot is also a good friend of India.'

'But he supported Mrs Gandhi during the emergency, didn't he?'

'Yes, but he is a good friend because he leads the Labour Party and Indians feel friendly towards the Labour Party because it was from them that they received independence. And there is Enoch Powell. I think I hate Enoch Powell. Yes, I do hate him, and he is a Conservative.'

'He has left the Conservative Party now.'

'I hate him.'

He had heard of Tony Benn but didn't know much about him, and he mentioned Harold Wilson.

Before I left he told me how to find my way to my next appointment. I showed him my map. His pen hovered over Connaught Place.

'We are here,' he said, marking the paper. 'You cross over this road and go up here or here. You could go this way. You want to go to here,' he vaguely waved the pen over a square two inches of the small-scale map. 'Go up here and turn right then ask any well-dressed person the way.'

'Thank you', I said. 'I'm sure I'll get lost.'

'No, no, it's very near.'

With many expressions of earnest hope that we'd meet soon in London, we said farewell and I trailed off into the night, determined not to panic when I got lost or start hurrying and get exhausted.

Actually I found my way very easily and although I did ask the way once from a tall Sikh who was very helpful, I only did it to confirm what I was already pretty sure of.

I got there so quickly I was a quarter of an hour early and sat outside a Sikh temple listening to some lovely singing that was being played over loudspeakers, watching people cooking on the pavement nearby and gazing at the people passing in and out of the floodlit temple. It was a peaceful, busy scene. Some stalls lit by candles were open and selling food. On the wall were some slogans painted in English and in a script unknown to me. One said: 'Sikhs will not tolerate injustice'; another, 'Why the same treatment to Sikh leaders and criminals?' I went to the house where I was expected. A doorman stepped out of the shadows and welcomed me.

'I was told you were arriving,' he said.

Here I spent a marvellous couple of hours with my hosts Mr Mangat Rai and his wife Nayantara Sahgal, drinking vodka and lime juice and talking. As usual I was made to feel quite at home and welcome, and conversation was easy and interesting and often funny. There were only two other guests.

A door leading to a balcony was open and a cool breeze gently billowed the sari of a beautiful woman sitting near it. Her husband talked about the economic side of the Festival of India. There was political gossip. I was asked about the inquiry into the Falklands war and what the chances were for the S.D.P. in the next few months. The evening could not have been more delightful.

'We would so much have liked to ask you to dinner,' said my hostess, 'but our cook had to go to see her parents or something, so . . .'

'I'm sorry, that would have been such a pleasure.'

Early morning, Delhi Station

Agra

Saturday 20th November

I have slept badly since I came here and this was the worst night so far. I asked for a call at 5.30 because I had to catch the 7.00 train for Agra and had been told to leave a good hour earlier to get to the station and find my seat and all that.

Downstairs I was surprised to see the same staff in the buffet, which is open twenty-four hours a day, as had been there the night before. The waiter grinned and said, 'Good morning, are you going to catch the Taj Express?'

'You still here?' I said.

'Yes sir, eight to eight.'

I realised that behind the glamorous luxury of this place there is some very hard work.

I got to the station shortly after 6.00 a.m. and had a look at India's famed railway life. The whole place was swarming with people, hundreds and hundreds of them. They were sitting, standing, sleeping, moving, some wrapped-up and some half-naked, old, young, men, women, jam-packed solid. The colour of the whole scene was dirty brownish-grey. Everything was extremely grubby. Most of the people were shrouded in cloaks; the ones that were asleep were completely wrapped up like corpses. There was more than a touch of the underworld about the scene; I felt there might be ghostly railway men waiting somewhere to shunt them across to the other side. There were patches of colour, particularly from the red turbans and jackets of the porters, one of whom grabbed my bag, put it on his head and loped off through the crowd.

Yet so rapid is the mind to adjust to new circumstances that I was not in the least downcast by the gloomy atmosphere of the station. On the contrary, it was another extraordinary experience, one I've seen arty photographs of in colour magazines and often read about, and it was exhilarating to find myself in it. Oddly, I was not moved to pity by the suffering of the people all round me, nor was I humbled by the thought of how awful life could be here if one was a bit unlucky. Instead I was anxious not to lose sight of my porter and keen to make sure I found my place in the train. I was beginning to get used to poverty and crowds and this spectacle, that would be flabbergasting anywhere in Europe, I found interesting, even amusing. That is to say I was very amused by a middle-aged couple, possibly American or German, standing and studying some papers—

Delhi Station

probably tourist brochures. They were so well dressed, so studiedly casual, so concentrating on their bit of paper, so ludicrously affluent amid the catastrophe all round them. Behind them stood a man in a Macy's lightweight suit, a thin check shirt from Brooks Brothers, and a silk tie: he was drawing them in a sketch book. That was me. And looking at me were a number of young Indians giggling and whispering; to them I was much funnier than the middle-aged couple. I drew some young men washing at a sink and added the face of an appalling beggar who was crouching at my feet with mad eyes and black skin.

I think one is protected to a very large extent from the impact of horrifying poverty by the practical need to survive it. In other words much of the concentration and concern that the spectacle of the hungry, ragged, miserable crowd demands is given over to making sure you pick your way through it safely. And another shield is the absolute certainty that there is nothing you can do about it. This anyway was my experience but I have often spoken to people who have returned from India depressed and upset by the poverty they have seen.

On the notice-board by the train that the porter had led me to was a list of names. I found mine. After it was written M47. Several other people were peering at the notice and I asked one, 'Is that the number of my seat?'

'No,' he replied, 'that's you: Male, forty-seven years old. It's so that I know who you are.' I saw that he was carrying papers and wore what could be a uniform of some sort.

'Your carriage is number nine,' he pointed, 'and your seat number three.'

'Thank you,' I said, and he smiled merrily.

A long, long train slid up to the platform. I found my place and left my bag, then walked about again on the platform. I watched a newspaper-and-book stall being set up. Two cloaked men did the work while a fat bully in a shirt shouted at them and occasionally hit one of them.

Delhi Station

Soon the train pulled out. First we passed urban squalor. There is a lot of life around an Indian railway. Whole families walked along beside the track or between the rails of a parallel line; I watched one little girl taking huge strides from sleeper to sleeper. We began to pass close to tent-cum-shanty towns. They were built right up to the edge of great pools of unbelievably nasty water: great, black, scummy lakes of filth. India had shocks left for me. Did I think, only a few minutes before, that I had adjusted to anything? Behind me a bright pair of young ladies with a rather spoilt little boy called Arun twittered and laughed with excitement as the train journey began.

'Be a good boy, Arun, and say "Hello" nicely, and perhaps he'll draw your photograph,' said one of them very loudly and archly.

'Hello Arun,' I said holding out a finger for him to take.

'Shake hands, Arun.' He looked away, not embarrassed but bored. The two women laughed and I shrugged at them smiling. A few yards away outside was hell.

The horror of what I saw in the damp early morning light has not left me. I don't mean it has permanently clouded my spirits or ruined anything, but it was an unforgettable sight—deeply moving and profoundly upsetting. Draped figures sat in the foul mud or slithered along towards some horrible spot on some unimaginable errand. Little children sheltered under decaying scraps of canvas. Could there really be a smile in this poverty, as Romesh had said? The colour of this scene was dark greyish-black and it was slimy.

Across the aisle a young American couple were reading books; now and then the man read aloud. It was a history of Agra and he was telling his wife about the Mogul Empire. Outside the window a man squatted, defecating, his bare bottom turned towards the train. Near him people walked by, both he and they completely unconcerned. On a wide open, rubble-strewn patch maybe five or six men were defecating. They were ten or twenty yards from each other and oddly unarranged; they neither faced nor turned from one another. It was as if they had stopped and squatted all at once, while in the act of walking in different directions. I wondered whether this was a regular early morning ritual or whether one had set the others off, as one yawn will begin several more.

The urban scene began to give way to more open country without very much improvement in the general standard of life. Crumbling factories appeared, and for many miles on every available brick wall armies of men had painted in huge white letters 'SAVE TIME AND MONEY BUY VICKY MINI MOTORS'. The word Vicky was painted in a different script to the rest and closely resembled the signature of the great cartoonist. The dot of the I was a horizontal dash for instance. I wondered whether somehow his name had been taken by the Mini Motor manufacturers.

The rural dwellings were often mud huts with bamboo roofs clustered together. Low dimly-coloured walls crumbled like sandcastles on the beach. The day was overcast and rain threatened; the land was damp and looked uncomfortable. The open country was dotted with palm trees and bushes and flat to the horizon. Here too the fields were full of men squatting for an early morning evacuation. I suddenly thought 'Hang on—no women?' Where or when did *they* do it? Could it be that they were shyer; more discreet? I have heard Jeff Bernard maintain many times that women neither fart nor shit. Could he be right after all . . .?

Not all I saw was depressing. The scene was often busy and matter-of-fact. There were farmers ploughing with simple ploughs pulled by pairs of bullocks. Elsewhere I saw tractors towing farm machinery. There were bright green birds in the trees; parrots I supposed. Way out in the country I saw a man in long flowing robes striding with bounding steps over a field and giving great waves of his arms, first left then right, to the speeding train. He may have been demented or just feeling terrific.

A line of women in red, gold, purple and yellow saris came down a muddy track under some trees each carrying a brass pot on her head, and looking quite lovely. There is something very beautiful about Indian clothes. Even a filthy blanket worn tossed over the shoulder has something of the shape of a dashing cavalry officer's uniform from early in the last century. A turban can give a man a noble and mysterious look even though he is very poorly dressed; and the folds of a loin cloth or robe are also beautiful. The women's clothes are superb. There can hardly be a sight in the world to compare with a good-looking Indian woman walking in a pretty sari. Their bodies are not hidden so much as hinted at by the flowing material, and the glimpse of bare midriff below their tight little bodices is extremely erotic. Their long black hair is usually parted in the middle and swept back into a pigtail; or left lying over the shoulders or pinned up at the back, and most wear a little red spot of make-up on their forehead. The deep dark red looks wonderful against brown skin and absolutely ghastly on a white forehead, like a pimple.

While the train was stopped at Mathura Station I watched a child in the churning crowd. She was not very old, perhaps thirteen, and was wearing a pale, nondescript sari. She was bent over, busy I thought at some task, when she suddenly straightened and gave a delightful hop forward, her sari flying out behind her. It was not a disgraceful example of child labour: she was playing hopscotch.

Mathura Station from the Taj Express

At one point in the journey (which takes about three and a half hours) a young German girl came and asked if she could take the seat next to mine. She was in her early twenties and neither pretty nor plain. She spoke excellent English and was friendly and charming. I was slightly irritated as she chattered on because I could not continue to gaze out of the window; good manners demanded that I didn't just turn my head away.

She had come to India because of her interest in mysticism. She had met some Indian students of German at home and was now staying with one in his student hostel in Delhi. Girls could stay in boys' hostels but boys could not stay in girls' hostels. She thought this was very wrong. Her host also had an Italian girlfriend from the Italian embassy. The girl, whose name I never discovered, had worked and saved for this trip and her mother had done everything she could to prevent it happening. She had wept and shrieked and tried to keep her daughter at home with hoops of guilt. This technique had failed dismally. Her father, who worked on the production line in a factory, had apparently had no views on the matter.

'Are you interested in mysticism?' she asked me.

'No, not at all I'm afraid!' She gave me that slightly soupy, pitying smile that would-be mystics tend to affect in the presence of non-believers. It is meant to let you know that they understand that insight has not been granted to you—yet. It is the smirk of a passenger on a full bus, zooming straight past a long queue, and I don't like it much. But I did not feel cross with her. I just smiled back.

I tried to explain why I was not interested as she pressed me to, but it was useless. She told me that the painter Albrecht Dürer was heavily into Tantra signs. 'No, really, you can see them all, there is a painting . . . Why are you laughing at me, you look so amused?'

She had got into a second-class compartment by accident and had spent the first part of the journey crushed together with about two thousand Indians and their luggage. 'It was awful!'

'Nothing mystical about that,' I said. She laughed, and told me to shut up.

The couple I'd noticed reading when I first got on the train only closed their books as we drew into Agra. I hadn't watched them all that closely but it seemed to me they had hardly glanced out of the window the whole way.

It started to rain just outside Agra and it changed the whole look of India. Wet poor people look very much worse off than dry ones.

I was picked up immediately by a guide and his young driver. My first task was to make sure I had a reservation on the train to Jaipur the next day, so I told the guide who took me to the reservation counter. The young German girl wanted to buy a ticket back to Delhi. She looked very lost in the big, pushing, heaving crowd. It turned out I had to go to a different station for my reservation.

'Thirty rupees,' screeched my guide, dribbling scarlet betel juice from his frightful mouth.

'O.K.,' I said. 'And back to the hotel.'

'Please back to hotel,' he agreed.

I felt vaguely that I shouldn't just leave the girl alone in this place, particularly as she probably couldn't afford a taxi. I saw her looking disconsolately at a long fighting queue in front of the ticket office, and then and there I decided, ungallantly, I just couldn't wait while she struggled through that lot. I swam over to her and said I was off to another station and did she want a lift. I think she considered for a moment just risking it and not bothering with a ticket, but she was a sensible and resourceful girl in spite of being a mystic, and she said no, she was going to wait and fix it up now. I admired her and thought she must be either quite tough or quite utterly daft to be doing all this on her own.

Out in the rain we went to the car and drove off splashing away down the road. I never really got the hang of Agra. It seemed to straggle dirtily all over the place. I never knew where I was and felt angry with the weather; would the Taj Mahal work, I wondered, in this dripping grey weather?

The guide told me it was thirty rupees for this journey and for another fifty I could have his car and services as a guide all day. I had done more or less no travel-reading at all, and didn't know what to do here; it was pouring with rain and I thought 'Oh, what the hell, O.K.'

We fixed up my reservation and I checked into the Sheraton. A brand new, comfortable, luxury hotel. It was arranged I'd have some lunch and take a trip to the Taj and the Red Fort and various other places at about half past one.

I was nervous about the Taj Mahal. I had wanted to see it for so long: it was so famous, so familiar. Everyone who has seen it raves about it. (Actually I know one man who drawled 'I found it disappointing' when I asked him about it before leaving England.) I had seen it from the windows of the hotel when I was having lunch. There it was through the trees, but that didn't count. As we drove to it the idiotic guide kept up a shrill inaccurate account of its construction and dates. Luckily it was also pretty incomprehensible as his toothless gums and mouth full of hellish red spit rendered speech pretty tricky. I wished he'd just shut up and I tried to look out of the window. I was feeling all wrong; not ill or anything definable. Just out-of-sorts.

We arrived and I bought a ticket. The car was going to wait for me. 'Take your time—an hour, an hour and a half,' drooled the guide. I passed through the gateway along with hundreds of others; Indian families pushing and chattering, Europeans all guide books, rucksacks and cameras, and Japanese determined, grim and spotlessly clean.

I stood on the steps of the gate-house, looked down the long reflecting pool at the Taj, and waited. Nothing happened. The rain had stopped and the crowds swirled all round me. I wondered what to do. In my imagination I had always seen myself alone at the Taj Mahal; photographs of it don't usually include tourists so I had not included them either. I thought miserably, 'It's not going to work. Perhaps I will have to lie about it or even worse tell the truth, that I found it disappointing.' So instead of going on I turned to the left and walked across a bit of lawn towards some trees. My attention was drawn to the sound of clinking hammers and I went to investigate. There were half a dozen stone-masons chipping away at gigantic flagstones, levelling them with chisels. They were wonderfully skilful. Puffs of stone rose with each rhythmic blow. The regular fall of the hammers didn't falter even when they looked up at me, curious to see who was visiting them.

I took out my sketch book and began a drawing. Several men who were not working got up to come and watch and I found, as I have discovered for the first time in this country, that having a good-natured interested audience, far from putting me off, unexpectedly makes drawing easier. By the time I was finishing a quick drawing all the masons had laid down their hammers and chisels and had also come to watch. When I wrote 'STONE-MASONS...' under the drawing one of them insisted, 'Red—red—red stone-masons,' so I added the word red and he nodded and smiled approvingly. They all shook hands with me, maybe ten or a dozen of them; and feeling much better I returned across the garden to stare again down the reflecting pool.

Red stone-masons, Taj Mahal

Although my mood had lightened the day was still grey and the sight was impressive rather than moving. As I set off towards the Taj the sun quite suddenly broke through the clouds and for a moment the whole garden and the great white building was drenched in golden light that almost at once faded again. I entirely forgot my anxiety and doubts. I had seen in those few seconds the breathtaking beauty of the Taj.

Later it occurred to me that the strong emotion I felt for the rest of the two and a half hours I wandered around and inside the building was not entirely unconnected with the shocking scenes by the railway I'd seen a few hours before. Examples of such sublime achievement and such degrading waste so swiftly juxtaposed had possibly unhinged me for a bit and left me more or less unable to control my feelings. Whatever it was I became more and more moved as I drew nearer to the Taj and the sun began to shine more strongly until it had cleared the sky altogether. I had not been prepared for the brilliant flowers made of semi-precious stones inlaid in the white marble or the words from the Koran in black. Neither did I know how richly carved and decorated is the whole building or how gently marked by time it is—the steps worn and the doorways smoothed by the passage of millions of visitors. Even here there are names scratched into the walls; written by those weird tourists who bother to come out to the place and then set about spoiling it. I asked a guide whether he'd ever seen anyone actually carving his name.

'Oh yes,' he said, smiling. 'Yes, yes, lots of them.'

'What do you do?' I asked, angered by his casual reaction.

'I arrest them,' he said, grimly clutching his arm suddenly to demonstrate. 'Yes, my officers arrest them.'

'What happens to them?'

'Fined two hundred, three hundred rupees, maybe more,' he said with satisfaction.

'Are you angry with them?'

'Yes, very angry and it is the educated ones you know. They can write,' he said in disgust. Some other guides were listening and smiling and nodding. He'd been a guide for twenty years, another for twenty-eight years.

'Do you grow tired of it?' I asked, somewhat ridiculously. 'Tired of it? Tired of the Taj? It's new,' said the twenty-eight-year man reverently. I felt very pleased that he too had played his part so well, and for all I knew he meant it.

I saw the German girl sitting on a wall with a couple. She looked very happy.

'Did you get your ticket O.K.?'

'Yes,' she said and waved her hand around. 'It's great, isn't it?'

The rest of the day passed in a haze. I was driven around some shops first. I was taken to a shop which sold marble inlay and sat down to behold some hideous boxes and plates and table tops. Well, all right, not hideous but very garish and crude. I sat slumped, doing my silent Indian act.

'Have you just been from the Taj?' asked the shopkeeper, like a doctor with a new, very worried, patient.

'Yes.'

'You feel very—er—it was very beautiful?'

'Yes, very, very beautiful. I feel a bit stunned.'

'Yes, you will feel like that for about two weeks,' he said.

In a jeweller's shop I listened to their hard sell for a bit and then said, 'Look, I'm sorry, I don't want any of this lovely work. I think it's very beautiful but it's not what I am looking for. Thank you,' and I tried to go.

'We've got plenty more; please, sit down, please, would you like some tea? Please. Look, isn't that nice? Madam would like that.'

I said no and then they got all hurt and redoubled their efforts. I sat back and said, 'Look, you are making me feel uncomfortable. I don't want to waste your time. You are being very kind and hospitable and I don't want to be rude or hurt your feelings, but I *don't want it*.'

I explained that English people might be irritated by this sort of pressure; they should be aware it might even drive people away. 'I hope you don't mind me talking like this?'

'Not at all,' grin, grin. 'We are very enlightened.' I really think they thought they had a nut-case on their hands; they listened attentively, not believing or perhaps not understanding a word.

'You might try a softer approach sometimes,' I blundered on. 'Just let people wander round, have a look, make up their own minds.' They continued to unpack more and more boxes of junk.

'This would look nice on madam.' It was all so practised. One part of me felt that they were actually quite contemptuous behind the elaborate concern and extravagant friendliness.

I bought a couple of cheap trinkets and as I left the shop it seemed to me that behind me the friendliness was abruptly switched off.

Next was the Red Fort. While I was aware of how beautiful and impressive it was, I was full. I couldn't really take any more. Years ago I discovered that the way to go to art galleries is to pick just a few pictures and look closely at them. Look at too many and you will have the visual or intellectual equivalent of eating too much. You will feel ill, or even sick it all up, neither enjoying it nor benefiting from it. So I didn't really look at the Red Fort. I walked in it and mused and considered things and rested.

In one out-of-the-way corner I looked into a great dim marble room and reeled back nauseated by the stench of old urine; tourists, I suppose, had used it as a lavatory. I was reminded of a conversation with a friend that took place in France some years ago after we had visited a château on the Loire. I had said, 'I wonder what it was like here in the old days,' as I looked round in a spotless roped-off room. 'They ought to keep one part of it as it was, just to let us see.'

'You wouldn't like it much if they did,' said my friend. 'In those days these weren't so much châteaux as shiteaux!' His words came back to me and amused me all over again as I retrospectively acknowledged he was right.

Police and two tourists at the Red Fort, Agra

I was exhausted. I sat for a while where Shah Jehan must have sat, and like him I gazed at the Taj Mahal across the river.

I went back to the hotel quite exhausted, but wrote letters to my boys before allowing myself to go and eat.

Sunday 21st November

All morning I wrote my journal. I am faced all the time by a difficult problem: do I cram in as much as I can while I have the opportunity or do I spend time recording and in a way digesting what I have seen and done already?

A hotel official put me in touch with a couple of English journalists who were staying at the hotel and we had coffee together; Makay from *The Guardian* and a girl from the North whose name I did not catch. They are both here doing travel pieces and are seeing a rather different India from mine. They have seen more sights and have travelled more widely than I have, but have not sat and talked quite so much perhaps. Makay was born in India and in a way doesn't need the basic contact I feel a great desire to make.

But it was interesting, as we talked, to feel how differently they were approaching the place. They were more confident travellers than I am and knew perfectly well what they had to do and how. I tend to become very easily moved or alarmed, but there is a cheerful, no-nonsense attitude that journalists acquire—they are bloody well going to look after themselves—that I envy and also dislike because it tends to cut them off a little from a kind of contact which is very rewarding.

They had arranged for someone from the tourist board to take them on a drive in the afternoon. They both had seen the Taj in the rain yesterday morning and wanted to return. Outside it was now a lovely hot day and we agreed to go together to the Taj first and they'd go on afterwards. I did not have time to accompany them in the drive, much as I would have liked to, because I had a train to catch at 5.30 for Jaipur.

Back in the gardens of the Taj Mahal I asked the tourist official whether it was possible to go down to the river bank to see a different view and he called a young man to show me the way. He also thought it was possible to take a boat across the river, but this turned out to be impossible, or anyway the boat was not there. On the way to the river we looked into the museum where I was very pleased to see portraits of Mumtaz Mahal and Shah Jehan, both extremely good-looking. It was something I had been missing without knowing it. I had no faces to put to the hero and heroine of the tragic story of this enchanting place.

Thinking about the Taj last night after I had written about it, I realised that I had not described the crowds of people who were there. No one ever does. The odd thing is they do not figure in one's memory although they are very much part of the experience. There is an amazingly resonant echo inside the Taj. The guides sing out a strange chanting call to demonstrate it, but, though they are urged not to, hundreds of squeaking children and baaing young men showing off also call and scream and shout and there is a permanent din inside, at least on a Sunday or touristy day. Outside millions of photographs are taken but there the crowd is dispersed over a large area and less oppressive.

Another thought that came to me was that although the Taj Mahal is famous for being quite different at different times of day there is another way in which it changes that I have never heard described. It is so built that you must first see it from a distance, because it is surrounded by an enormous high-walled garden in very flat country. You do not come across it suddenly round a corner. Consequently you are bound to see it as a miniature on first aquaintance. You can see its domes and minarets all in one glance, and enjoy the perfect symmetry and balance of the whole. As you draw nearer it is transformed and becomes almost unimaginably huge. It soars into the sky, vast and uncontainable; its domes disappear behind its great sheer walls and you feel awed by the grandeur of its conception. But at the same time you begin to see the glittering inlaid semi-precious stones and the wonderfully carved flowers, and in black marble round the entrance holy words from the Koran, so it is a thousand miniatures even while it is a colossal whole. This quality the building has of being many things that shift and change unexpectedly is disturbing and marvellous. It is at the same time a great monument to grief and loss and a symbol of permanence, unchanging and glorious.

I walked round the Shah Jehan gardens with my guide and together with a gardener we visited a nursery garden behind the walled rose-garden. Here were many plants and shrubs, sprinkled with water from overhead pipes and shaded by a roof of bamboo slats. I asked for a flower to press to send to my wife and was given a large bouquet of roses and many other blooms with names unknown to me. I pinned a sweet-smelling yellow rose on my lapel. I eventually gave most of the flowers to one of the hotel men who told me later he gave them to a little girl guest. I hope she liked them.

On the way out I passed the stone-masons who grinned and waved at me.

Later, talking to the hotel official to whom I gave the flowers, I learnt more about the stone-masons. He said they are extraordinarily skilled and highly paid too. Furthermore they will only work when they feel like it. I remembered how they'd all downed tools to come and look at me. 'If they don't feel like working they don't. Even if you were to offer them two lahks (200,000 rupees) to just finish off a little job, they would ignore you.'

The man asked to see my sketch book and told me more about the *hijra*. They may be born neither male nor female but with both sex organs. 'Like a sex-change person,' explained another man who was listening. 'Or sometimes they have been cruelly mutilated as children. They seem to just know when there is going to be a wedding or a celebration and they just turn up. Also they sometimes take children.'

'Do you mean *hijra* children or normal children?'

'Normal children and mutilate them.'

'Are you sure?'

'I've heard it; people are nervous of them. They will surround people and pester them and pester them until they have to give money.'

'But,' I asked, 'don't people dislike them, for stealing children?'

'They do not respect them,' he answered. 'They have no status, no prestige, they cannot have. They are outcasts. If they are frustrated or angered they may become a bit obscene.' He dropped his voice and for the first time became embarrassed, giggling and covering his mouth with his hand. 'They will show you their—er—awful—um—private parts. There are ladies present,' he added, indicating a girl behind the counter near where we were standing. She caught my eye and smiled serenely.

I got to the station in plenty of time and found my place in the first class compartment. It was dirty—I mean filthy—and dark and fairly hot. I had had a picture in my mind of Indian rail travel being comfortable, old-fashioned and rather splendid. It is old-fashioned but neither comfortable nor splendid; at least this train wasn't.

Agra Station

Some silent young men stared at me from the hard bench the other side of the compartment. I did a drawing of a beggar sitting on the ground outside. I did not want to leave my bag in order to stroll on the platform because I have heard you can be robbed.

After a bit a young European couple entered the compartment and looked around; the man, somewhat aggressively.

'Did you book this place?' he said.

'Yes,' I replied.

'Whose are these things?' He pointed to some bags the Indians had left behind while they walked outside.

'There were some young men here a moment ago.'

'Right, they'll get the order of the boot,' said the man.

I thought they were Australians from their language but they turned out to be Welsh. Steve and Christine were their names.

During the journey we talked about our experiences. They were on a five-week holiday which they had planned for some time. They usually went fairly far afield for their holidays: they had been to Sicily, Greece, Turkey and so on, but had always longed to visit India.

'Several times,' they said ruefully, 'we have been on the point of just going home. We've had a hard time.'

They described endless battles with railway and aeroplane bookings, third-rate hotels with rats and cockroaches, tummy upsets and exhausted lugging-of-luggage round from place to place. They were driven mad by Indians trying to get their money by offering unrequired services; or if required, not satisfactorily completed. They had been badgered by requests to sell things.

'Some bloke wanted to buy my socks,' said Steve with incredulous laughter. 'That was after I'd told him I didn't want to sell my watch, my camera, my bag or my other clothes!'

They said, 'India is supposed to be a cheap country but we've already spent a thousand pounds and we've got two weeks to go. We've had to use our credit cards. There are four of us but our friends can't come with us to Agra. The wife of my friend is ill.'

'What's wrong with her?'

'Dunno. We've all had it once or twice. Christine had it in Calcutta. We got aches all over, fever, sore throat, headache and some sickness. It was pretty awful.'

It turned out that they found the water purifiers they had bought made the water taste so horrible they had drunk unpurified water in restaurants.

I expressed amazement at their foolhardiness.

'Yeah, well, we drink bottled drinks now but our friends say it's silly and that they'll get used to the water soon. Apparently, you *can* get used to it.'

I thought they all sounded nuts and the unfortunate friends slightly nuttier than Steve and Christine.

The other thing that was obvious to me was that they were trying to see too much. They had already crossed India from Calcutta to Delhi and been by train to Darjeeling and Benares on the way. They were doing Rajasthan, Bombay and Goa and back to Delhi before flying home.

'When you thought of going home what stopped you?' I asked.

Steve thought a bit. 'It was just too much hassle to change the schedules I think,' he said.

Their whole experience differed from my own. One thing that occurs to me (and I must ask someone about it) is that I have been going around dressed in a lightweight suit and I have worn a tie every day and carried a smart bag with my drawing equipment in it; I look like a gent, as an Indian had told me, so obviously people don't ask to buy my socks and perhaps they treat me generally differently.

I have also had the benefit of travelling on expenses rather than on my own money and, even more valuable, I've had rooms in good hotels, back to which I have retired from time to time to bathe, change, rest and refresh myself. The hotels have also advised me, made calls for me, put their services at my disposal, and been interested in having a cartoonist drawing their dining rooms and lawns.

All this has meant that although we've been in the same places we've seen different things.

Christine leant forward at one point. She was a slim, shy-looking girl; she was neatly dressed and carried a red bag.

'I would do it again,' she said quietly, 'even knowing what it would be like. It has been hard but it's also been so—interesting . . .' Her voice trailed off. I admired her stoical attitude. They both agreed that it had been a rewarding experience, however hard it had been.

The only thing they did that annoyed me was that when at one station the Indians all left, they locked the compartment door.

An Indian family, two women, a man and several children, noticed the half-empty compartment from the platform and tried the door a few moments later. Steve and Christine smiled, satisfied.

'Oh, let them in,' I said. I was looking forward to trying to make friends with the children. Neither of them moved. The family got off the train and, looking sourly through the windows, passed by to sit elsewhere.

There was a silence and then Christine undid the lock. Soon two huge policemen and a railway official came in and sat down next to Steve and I got a cruel satisfaction at seeing him worse off than he would have been with the children as travelling companions.

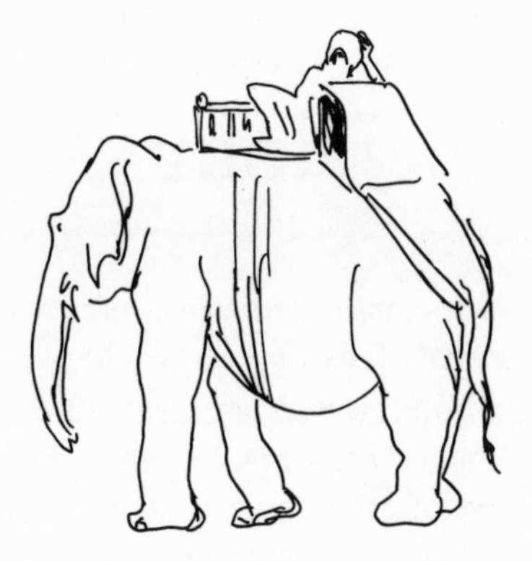

Elephants at Amer, near Jaipur

Jaipur

At Jaipur I found a porter and shot off, leaving Steve and Christine in the crowd. I was grotesquely overcharged by the taxi driver, but the hotel was so wonderful I really didn't care.

The Rambagh Palace Hotel is just that. It is a Maharajah's Palace and it's made of marble. It is surrounded by lawns and flowerbeds and trees, and I don't think there is a better hotel in the world.

I had a bath in a marble bathroom and ordered some food and drink. That wasn't too good actually, because it was so late that the kitchen was closed and the sandwiches they sent up were a bit dry and small; but the lime soda was terrific. I wrote for hours.

Monday 22nd November

I wrote in the morning until hunger drove me downstairs to breakfast. In the daylight the hotel is even better because of the wonderful views of the garden; and there are the places to sit in the sun or under cool marble arcades. The dining room is quite splendid with huge green double doors.

After breakfast I took a taxi into the old town. As soon as I was dropped at the gates I cursed myself for not arranging to stay longer. It is the prettiest, the most charming, the busiest and most picturesque place imaginable. It is really one huge bazaar, with scores of side streets filled with stalls and shops. It has happened very often that I have turned up at a place that has been closely described to me and found that although it fits the description well, it still comes as a complete surprise. It may be much worse, like the Central Reservation Office in Delhi or it may be much better, like the old city in Jaipur.

I did a drawing of a decorated doorway. Among the crowd that came to watch me was a little girl of five or so with her slightly older sister. I began to put her into the drawing and the crowd of young men watching me rocked with laughter. The two little girls realised I was drawing them and fled. I tried to grab the little one to look at the dress she was wearing in order to draw the pattern but she was too quick. The laughter increased and then became even merrier when a little boy of about ten stepped forward to where the little girl had been and posed for me, looking piercingly at me with an enormous fixed grin.

In Daracloth Market, Jaipur

When I packed up and moved on an older boy of perhaps fifteen followed me. He had been very talkative while I was drawing, speaking quite good, but halting English, with a strong accent. When I stopped at a shop he began acting instantly as a sort of interpreter, which was not necessary. He was very insistent that we went this way or that and kept saying, 'Please, what you want? You want "clothe-ez" (I don't know if he meant clothes or cloth), you can come to my shop. Please?' I wandered on mostly ignoring him and he tagged along. Gradually I found I was asking him things and talking to him, but actually found him a bit of a pest. I quite admired his persistence though. After a while he said, 'Sir, I think you are merciful man.'

'Oh? What do you mean?'

'Sir, you are a merciful man; give me your pen!'

'Give you my pen?'

'Yes, please. I am a student. Give me your pen.' His head tilted to one side in a gesture of passive pleading.

'No, I won't,' I said. 'I need it.'

'Please. I am a student. *I* need it.'

'No; anyway you can't get ink for it.' I explained about the cartridges he'd need which are not available here.

'We have ink in India.'

'I know you do, but you can't have my pen.'

'I could have stayed at my shop and made a lot of money,' he said, looking fed-up, almost begging.

'You want money?' I said. 'O.K.,' and gave him five rupees. 'Now you can go back to your shop.' But he didn't go. He kept pace with me. After a bit he said, 'My brother will ask me where do you live?'

'Tell him I live in London.'

Silence. Then, 'My brother, my elder brother will ask me, where do you live? He will be angry with me when I go back to my shop.'

I realised what he meant. His brother would tick him off for not being at the shop.

'Then go back to your brother.'

'Please, you are merciful man—pen.'

'No.'

By this time I had done a bit of shopping. The best place was a marvellous toy shop. All the toys were made of brilliantly-coloured wood. Soldiers, animals, little wooden figures of gods, beads, model cooking things and so on. I bought lots and lots of them. I love them. While the shopkeeper was packing them up I drew him and he looked very pleased when he saw the drawing. He went and got a large plaster figure of Ganesh and set him up on the floor and asked me to draw him. When I had done the drawing he smiled and wrote *Ganesh* in Hindi on the page. Then he joined his hands flat together and bowed slightly.

Figure of Ganesh in Jaipur toy shop

My little boy, whose name was Ajay, was carrying my parcels, but I was getting very tired of him.

'If I give you a pen will you go back to your brother?'

'Yes please.'

'I can't give you this pen,' showing him my No-Nonsense fountain pen, 'because I need it.'

'Yes please pen.'

'But I'll give you this one,' I said, taking out a fibre-tipped pen someone had given me. He took it morosely and opened it.

'No nib,' he said gesturing at my pocket.

'No, sorry; do you want it?'

'Yes please.'

'O.K., now go back to your brother.'

'I could have made lots of money at my shop.'

'Well, you'll know better next time,' I said, smiling at his cheek. Abruptly all his attention was switched off. No more smiles, no thanks, no goodbyes; he'd got what he could get and decided to jack it in. This sudden change of attitude, which always comes at the end of these little dealings with guides and shopkeepers in India, however much you've bought or however little, never fails to surprise and mildly hurt me. I have enjoyed the conversation and perhaps warmed to the individual a little and therefore I am polite and friendly; but they are utterly bored unless there is something in it for them. This doesn't apply to the friendly mobs watching me draw but then that whole relationship starts out on a different footing.

In the heart of the old town is the Maharajah's Palace, in a part of which the present Maharajah still lives. It is rather large. Near it is the strange observatory built by Maharajah Jai Singh in the 18th century and restored in the nineteen twenties. It has the look of an exhibition of modern abstract sculpture, which may partly be due to the restoration. It is a remarkable place with a de Chirico-like beauty. As you climb and turn through the strange marble and stone instruments you are endlessly presented with unexpected and pretty panoramic views of the crowd and gardens below, which amused me because these strange constructions were built to look the other way, upwards at the stars.

The observatory at Jaipur

I sat in a wide open courtyard-like part of the observatory and did some drawings. While I drew, a young man came and sat near me on some steps. He was much smoother and more urbane than most of the people I've met casually in the street. He professed to know a great deal about Jaipur because he had trained to be a guide, but he told me he'd eventually gone to Europe instead. He reeled off a list of European capitals and cities, in a curiously boastful and unconvincing way. 'Then I went back to Basle—I had to see a girl in Geneva—back to Naples with my other girlfriend . . .' and so on. It was all girls and travel but he was unforthcoming about any details of what he was actually up to apart from suggesting that it was one extended sexual adventure. He couldn't remember where he had lived in London for example.

I asked him where I could buy simpler peasant jewellery of a kind I had not seen in any shops. He said he knew an old man who broke up old jewellery to make new pieces. Would I like to visit him? I did not trust or like this fellow, who seemed to get such a kick out of talking about lingam worship and how Europeans didn't understand it. 'Of course they think it means worshipping a man's penis but it has a symbolic meaning they do not understand.' I wondered whether to go with him or not. When I discovered it meant a five-kilometre ride on his motorbike I decided against the idea. It was difficult to extricate myself from this invitation without being rude, but I said I was going to look at the Palace first and then maybe if there was time . . .

'I'll wait,' said Lothario.

I went to the art gallery, where I met Steve and Christine again, indefatigably sight-seeing, and looked at a large number of ancient Indian miniatures and decorative paintings. There was not much of the more primitive bolder work that particularly interests me, but one or two portraits and a picture of a woman swinging a baby up in the air struck me as particularly beautiful.

As I was leaving I saw some extremely delicate and lovely

paper cut-outs. They were very small and marvellously clever. The fine white paper was stuck down on prettily coloured card so that the picture appeared in colour. I looked at them for a long time. One was of a centaur-like creature pursued by a hunter. It was so like a Picasso drawing I could hardly believe my eyes. It was not dated but looked quite old—a hundred to a hundred and fifty years perhaps—but there was no way of telling. I stopped a busy-looking man who was passing and asked him whether he knew if it was possible to buy cards or photos of these remarkable little cut-outs. 'I'll remember your request and try to have some made,' he replied.

It turned out that I had accosted the head keeper of the Decorative Arts and Arms at the museum. He invited me to tea and led the way to his office. It was on the ground floor and splendidly large. The windows were shaded by a veranda outside and the comfortably cool and dim interior was cluttered with books and furniture and papers.

He had studied at the Metropolitan Museum of Art in New York and was an interesting man. We had a very pleasant talk. He told me there was an excellent book on Kalighat painting and he'd find me its name. He also promised to send me some photographs of one or two of the paper cut-outs.

Our conversation was cut short by a telephone call from the Maharajah who wanted him, so he had to go. His last visitor before me was a lady from Sothebys in London whom I had missed by a few minutes.

I said I hoped I had not ruined his lunch-hour.

'I never eat lunch,' he said. 'My father always said to me, "Son, eat lunch before you leave your house in the morning," and I do. At lunchtime I may have a cup of tea or something.' He was a round, solidly-built man, and I guessed he would eat a sustaining breakfast and perhaps a good dinner. I too think it is better to avoid lunch, or to have only a bite to put off pangs of hunger. A big lunch can wreck the rest of the day.

On leaving the Palace I got slightly lost trying to find my way back to the main road. I wanted to buy a bag for my purchases, as my travelling bag was now too full and would take no more. A bicycle rickshaw boy cycled along beside me talking and laughing and urging me to step into his vehicle and at last I did. I stopped and bought a bag with a lock and was cycled back to the hotel. It's not very comfortable in a bicycle rickshaw but it is a pleasantly slow way of travelling.

Before leaving the hotel to catch my train to Udaipur, I made an effort to book a hotel there which I had been unable to do from Delhi. I talked to the helpful and informative travel agent in the hotel and asked him how long the train journey from Udaipur to Aurangabad and on to Nagpur would take. He wrinkled his nose and thought for a bit and said, 'Well, you can't really do it by train. You could go Udaipur to Bombay and from Bombay to Nagpur, but to do it by local trains would take—oh—perhaps two and a half days, maybe more!'

I could not at first believe it. If it was true it ruined my schedule and would be a fearfully difficult and uncomfortable journey, with God knows what hazards, drinking and eating and maybe sleeping at local stations. I thought hard. The solution was obvious and not difficult to discover. Do not take the train to Udaipur, stay one more night here in lovely Jaipur and return to Delhi tomorrow by road. From Delhi take the express to Nagpur. The only possible catch would be if the hotels were full in Delhi because of the Asian Games; I did not want to finish up in too awful a place. I remembered that Romesh had said he could have got me into the India International Centre.

I rebooked into the hotel, bought a ticket for the coach ride back to Delhi and rang Romesh. No answer. I was not worried. I was so relieved to have discovered that my train journey was impossible before I'd gone too far to get out that I felt quite elated. And anyway the comforts of the Rambagh Palace were irresistible.

I went to have dinner in the marvellously elegant and grand dining room. To my surprise it was full and the head waiter said I'd have to wait for half an hour.

'I'll die of hunger,' I said.

'Would you mind sharing a table with someone?'

'Not in the least, providing of course that they don't mind.'

A moment later I was sitting down to dine with Malcolm McNeall, an Australian, in his fifties I'd guess, and a successful businessman. He had suddenly decided a week ago, '... to bloody well take off on a holiday.' He left his family and flew to India and was travelling around by himself on some sort of tour. He was having a great time and was full of cheerful tales of difficulties he had overcome and wonderful experiences he had had.

'I don't mind roughing it a bit, y'know, Nick,' he said, describing a hard overnight train journey. 'I just use my overnight bag as a pillow and go to sleep.' He knows the East quite well because he used to work as an engineer in Malaya, 'When it was still Malaya.' He had conceived the most profound respect for the abilities and honesty of his Chinese workmen, and considerable contempt for the Indians; 'Y'know, I reckon they're pretty good—at talkin'.' He had also known Singapore and Calcutta as a young man. I told him about Steve and Christine and he was sympathetic. 'Yeah! well, you wouldn't expect them to know how to handle it, would you. I mean comin' from Europe. It would seem a bit rough.' He obviously thought the Poms were a bit soft. He said that he thought Australia had a lot of problems and that unemployment was growing.

'It's going to mean big trouble soon.'

'What kind of trouble? Union trouble, crime wave, riots?'

'No, not the unions, I mean riots more. Y'know when a man hasn't got a job he gets pretty fed up.' He said to me, 'By the way, Nick, did you see the Taj Mahal?'

'Yes, I did.'

'What did you think?'

'I thought it was marvellous.'

'So did I, Nick. You know I never reckoned it much before. I mean, I'd heard of it and I knew what it looked like, but I dunno, I suppose I thought "well I'd better take a look at it," so

I did.' He leaned forward to emphasise his next words, which he pronounced with slow clarity.

'I reckon it was beautiful! I reckon it must be about one of the most beautiful buildings in the whole world—probably ever.'

'I absolutely agree,' I said. 'For me it was the high spot of my visit so far.'

'Oh, for me the high spot was Kashmir. You can really relax there.'

He gestured towards some musicians who were playing on a raised platform near where we were sitting. 'There's a subject for you,' he said. I drew the three musicians who noticed and smiled and nodded at me. Malcolm watched over my shoulder, muttering, 'Oh, that's great,' and giving little grunts of satisfaction.

When I'd finished, the musicians asked to see the drawing and I passed it to them. They laughed and pointed at it and gave it back. Malcolm and I applauded their playing.

Musicians at the Rambagh Palace Hotel, Jaipur

Tuesday 23rd November

In the morning I telephoned Romesh again, but the operator said she was getting no reply. I thought I'd try Arun and perhaps ask him to ask Romesh to fix something. I got through to Arun straight away and heard his high clear voice. 'Hello Nick, how are you?' I began to explain but almost before I started, 'You stay with us,' Arun interrupted. 'Oh Arun, I didn't mean to . . .' 'You stay with us, it is no trouble. We have a spare room. What time will you arrive?'

I was more pleased than I could say and the anticipation of a stay with the Shouries was enough to make me quite high for the rest of the day. I was also increasingly glad to have the opportunity to do more sightseeing in Delhi, a city for which I am beginning to realise I have developed a considerable affection. My surprise at finding the city so clean and tidy and beggarless seems to be shared by most Indians. The government ordered a huge clean-up for the opening of the Games and that's why it looks so good at the moment.

I spent the whole of the day lazing around pretending to be a rich playboy from the mid nineteen twenties, a fantasy not difficult to sustain in the Rambagh Palace. I sat and wrote in the shade of a vast marble porch. On the lawn in the sun a musician played and sang. English voices floated gently in the still hot air. I drank lime juice and soda and wrote a letter to Caroline. I heard a man explaining to a friend that his daughter seemed to have a gyppy tummy; he was looking for aspirins. I offered him some and told him I also had some codeine phosphate if that would be more help. The middle-aged gentleman thanked me and said if all else failed he'd come and ask me. We were wonderfully polite and formal with each other. Later he came back to say his daughter was better. In the course of the conversation I revealed that I worked for the *Telegraph*.

'Oh,' he said, 'we get the *Telegraph*. What do you write for them?'

'I'm the cartoonist,' I said. 'I do the political cartoon.' I waited smugly for cries of pleasure and interest.

'Oh really,' he said. 'I must look out for them.'

He took the opportunity to complain to me about falling standards of English. 'Particularly on the B.B.C., but even in the *Telegraph*. Do you talk *to* me or *with* me?'

'*To* you,' I replied smartly.

'Of course you do, you can't talk *with* me. You can walk *with* me and I can talk *at* you,' he said with a piercing look, 'but you cannot talk with me.'

'No,' I said.

'Well, that's the sort of thing I have to keep telling my daughter,' he said, frowning.

'Well,' I said, 'I'm not much of an expert, but language does change a bit all the time doesn't it? Fashions change, usage alters?' I faltered under his stern look.

Swimming pool, Rambagh Palace Hotel, Jaipur

I strolled in the garden and picked up some peacock feathers. I went to look at the indoor swimming pool. Hockney should visit this most lovely place. The absolutely mirror-like water reflected perfectly the Maharajah's swimming toys, the diving boards, slides and swings suspended over the pool from the high roof on long white ropes. Wicker chairs were arranged round the edge; there were Ladies' and Gentlemen's changing rooms and a bar. I did a drawing or two, sitting in the cool light filtering in through coloured glass windows.

At lunch in the restaurant the musicians from last night were playing again. One, playing the thamlla, managed to signal to me, 'Draw us again', even while his hand pounded away on his drums. So I did. When they had finished they all came over and shook hands. I took their names and the names of the instruments and resolved to send them at least a copy of my drawings.

Afterwards, as I waited for a taxi outside the hotel a cyclist, looking like any other cyclist, approached me. He was wearing a nondescript jersey and old trousers. I did not recognise him at first. It was the flute player. Gone were his lovely green and gold turban and his embroidered white cotton jacket and short trousers tight at the calf. He muttered away in Hindi (a waiter had told me he was illiterate and spoke no English). I heard the word 'artist' repeated several times. I pointed at myself queryingly. He nodded and said 'England, England?'

'Yes, I come from England.'

'Tape recorder,' he said beseechingly.

'Tape recorder?' His head went over on one side and his eyes looked appealing. I do not mean attractive, I mean begging. He joined his hands together and lowered his eyes.

'Yes,' he whispered. 'Tape recorder.'

'A tape recorder is very expensive.'

'Yes,' he said fervently. '*Very* expensive tape recorder.'

'Twelve hundred rupees,' I said, signalling with my hands.

'Yes, I send you,' he said softly.

'After I send *you* the tape recorder, you send *me* money?'

'Yes please.'

I looked at his shabby clothes and old bike. 'Well, I'll see what I can do.'

I got to the bus depot early and did a quick water-colour drawing of a policeman in a red and black turban dozing in the sun.

I noticed when the bus arrived that one of the double back tyres on the near side was stripped right down to the stitching. Great hunks of rubber hung off it. It was a dreadful sight. A man looked at me noticing it and smiled. I said, 'That would be illegal in England, very illegal indeed.'

'Nothing is illegal in India,' he said with a weary smile, 'if you can get away with it.'

'It doesn't look as if it will last a hundred yards,' I said.

'It'll last to Delhi,' he answered confidently.

'Oh well,' I thought, 'there's two of them. If one goes the other may hold.'

In fact, we changed buses for a more comfortable one at Amer. The journey was not too bad: there were one or two screeching halts as we nearly slammed into an unlit camel cart or a parked lorry. I slept and had disturbing, troubled dreams that lasted a few minutes until a swerve or bump brought me awake again. I was sitting alone and had no conversation.

Refreshment stop on Jaipur–Delhi bus

I was put down at about 10.00 at night near the district or place called Vasant Vihar and the bus pulled away. I was surrounded by half a dozen scooter-taxi drivers. They wore scarves wrapped around their heads against the chilly night air. One or two were wearing blankets as well.

I told them where I wanted to go and one decided he'd take me although he seemed only to have a vague idea of where we were heading. In fact, he got there quite soon, having woken a couple of dozing night watchmen who were sitting in chairs outside their masters' garden gates. Not every gate had a watchman but Arun's did. As the taxi stopped an old man in a black jacket with his head covered by a scarf stepped out of the shadows. He had a gun on his shoulder. He took my bags, gesturing me to leave them for him. I paid my driver and followed the old guard. I noticed that the barrel of his ancient gun was stuffed with cotton wool.

Inside the house I was shown upstairs to a lovely room and left alone. I could hear no sound. I wondered what to do. Arun had said they'd be in, but perhaps they went to bed very early. I began to tiptoe downstairs to look around and met Arun coming out of his sitting room.

'There you are. Did you have a good journey? Come in, come in.'

In the sitting room were his beautiful wife, Anita, his father and two journalists, Edward Behr and another, an American, whose name I did not catch.

I was offered food but took only a whisky and soda which was just what I wanted. We talked comfortably for an hour or so before the visitors left. Anita showed me my private bathroom and said, 'Be quite at home. We will be up around seven, but you can get up when you like.'

I washed and got into bed, and slept really well for the first time since I arrived in India.

Arun Shourie and Romesh Thapar

Wednesday 24th November

I woke early, before 7.00. It was wonderful to be in a house; in an Indian's house at that. Hotels have the effect of disorientating me in a way I cannot quite describe. Too long in any hotel or even series of hotels and I yearn for a touch of the real world, where not everything has a price and even the friendliness of the staff is part of the service. I do not mean Indian hotels—any hotels anywhere . . .

I went downstairs. There was someone in a room to my right; I could hear the faint noise of kitchen work. I went to the sitting room. If no one was there I was going to look through Arun's books and then get my journal to start writing. I had barely begun going along a bookshelf when Arun came in.

'You're up early! I thought you'd sleep for hours. Would you like coffee?'

A servant was hovering by the door and disappeared at once. The presence and work of servants in houses and offices creates a special sort of tempo to these occasions. There is no rush, no difficulty, no interruption to the conversation as there would be in England. 'Hang on, I'll just put on the kettle, back in a minute . . .' and all that sort of thing.

Arun and I sat down in the comfortable sitting room. The talk was instantly about India, politics and Mrs Gandhi. All the time I spent with Arun, when he was not playing very affectionately with his son or courteously complimenting me on my drawings or fixing up a meeting for me, he was talking politics in one way or another— to me, to Romesh, to Raj (Rom's wife), to various visitors or to people on the phone.

He began this morning with tales of government corruption and murder.

'Arun, do you really mean *murder*?'

'Oh, yes. It's really very common. It's not called that in the newspapers, of course—it's usually called "Dacoit shot in police raid" or perhaps "Naxalites gunned down in police battle."' (He explained that 'Naxalites' means belonging to a left-wing organisation which is named after its place of origin in West Bengal.) 'They just say you're a Naxalite, but I know cases where a man was taken away by the police. He called out to people who he was and what was happening and two days later it was announced he'd been shot in a battle with police. Everyone knew he'd been in police custody for two days.'

'How do *you* know this?'

'People come to me. There have been three thousand and twenty-five people killed in the last two and a half years in Utta Pradesh alone. These killings have a name: they are called "encounters". What happens is that perhaps a farm worker tries to organise labour into a union—he is taken away and shot. Or perhaps someone merely offends the police. Recently a tourist stopped his car to buy water. While he was gone some policemen came and molested his wife. He came back and was furious with them and shouted. They went away. A few moments later they came back and shot him.'

'Was there no enquiry; no court case?'

'Nothing.'

'I can't believe it.'

'It's difficult to believe, but it's true.'

I remembered a week ago someone saying Sanjay was a murderer, and I began to put that remark into a context. I said, 'If we went now to say a university campus and chose ten students at random and asked them, "Do you believe these stories?" what would they say? Do they know what's going on?'

'Yes, they know. You could ask thirty, or three hundred—

you would not find one who did not know. Not one.'

'Does *everyone* know?'

'Yes.'

'Does no one believe the press reports of dacoit shootings?'

'Sometimes real dacoits are shot, of course, but no one would be sure just by reading a report in a paper. They know many of these shootings are political murders.'

'And you published these stories?'

'Yes. These stories and others of corruption, fraud.'

'What happens?'

'The government denies it. They say I'm lying. I produce evidence—letters, signatures, dates of meetings, papers, photographs. Sometimes the government is forced to admit mistakes.'

'Does all this mean you are watched; put under surveillance by the government?'

'I was, during the emergency and afterwards for a while. Not now I think. Then my phone was tapped. People brought me tapes of my own conversations. They said "Why are you saying these things on the telephone? We are listening to every word".'

'Who were these people?'

'Officials who were angry with the government. They thought it was wrong.'

'Did they take a risk coming to see you?'

'Yes. Many Indians live at subsistence level. Their job is their lifeline. Suppose they lose their jobs or get posted to Nagaland—the back of beyond—they're finished . . .'

'Why don't I read about this sort of police atrocity, or government corruption in English papers?'

'I think foreign correspondents are lazy and Indian journalists are watching their jobs. There is a kind of community that journalists belong to and it's perhaps difficult to break out of it. Mrs Gandhi herself is enormously skilful at charming and impressing foreign journalists. She looks so aristocratic and she is so gracious. She does her homework, says the right thing, has the right books lying around. When the poor fellow leaves she reverts to her real self. "Take this rubbish away", she says.' (Here Arun flicked a cloth across the room to show how the literature and props of the interview are then discarded.) 'An Indian journalist's principal subject is government, his principal source of information is government and his principal audience is government. I tried to make my principal subject the people, my principal source the people and my principal audience the people.'

He went on, 'You will see a big headline after a Mrs Gandhi speech, "MRS GANDHI FOR PEACE". It's nonsense, absolute rubbish; what's she going to say? "Let's have a war"? This sort of journalism belongs in the small ads—"Education Minister still for Education".' He laughed, throwing back his head and narrowing his eyes. He is very handsome with fine features and thick black hair. He wears a clipped moustache. He looks like a cross between the young Douglas Fairbanks and the young Groucho Marx. He is slim and slightly-built and very neat in his movements.

'If you are known to attract anti-government informers and if you go right ahead and publish the stories, why does Mrs Gandhi tolerate you?'

'In the end she didn't,' he said simply, meaning 'In the end she has had me fired'. He continued, 'There is a second part to the answer. You see there is the democratic tradition here. It is still a very powerful force. Why did she call an election after the emergency? She didn't have to, but she wanted to. If she shuts me up she flies in the face of that tradition. She wants to look like a liberal and a democrat although she has the instincts and desires of a dictator.'

Another time Arun told me that he had been advised to have a guard during the emergency. Mrs Gandhi was anxious that nothing should happen to him because whether or not she had been responsible for his murder or injury, the entire country would believe that his blood was on her hands.

'If writing in Indian papers has become impossible, at least for the time being, why don't you write for foreign papers? Write in England or the U.S.A.?'

He leant forward and spoke unusually quickly.

'No, the moment I write anything abroad she will say, "There you see, that bastard has foreign masters who pay him to blackguard India overseas".'

'I knew it wouldn't last forever,' he said. 'I had a wonderful platform and I used it for as long as it was possible. But I have other interests; other things to do. I have books to write. I always said this, so that when they said to me "We'll take your job from you," I just said, "Take it—it means little to me".' He waved a hand dismissively.

'Your proprietor, who has now fired you, was himself a doughty warrior against Mrs Gandhi. After all he printed your stuff. What happened?'

'That's quite true. He is an extraordinary man. But he is getting old now, and they got at him through his family who are ignorant, stupid people and they put a lot of pressure on him. You know perhaps my real crime to him was that I had become too associated with the newspaper. People said "*The Express*? You mean the paper Arun Shourie writes for?"'

I asked him his views on the effect of Sanjay's death on Mrs Gandhi. He gave me a reply not unlike the one I'd heard a week before.

'She was liberated by his death. She was shattered for a time, but was liberated. In our country power is going into the hands of the criminals and gangsters. Sanjay personified that. We are entering the period of the robber barons.'

Arun spoke of this recent dramatic development in his career without becoming excited and remained thoughtful and good-natured throughout. He has a habit of closing his eyes and resting his hand on his forehead when he is thinking or trying to remember something which gives him a melancholy look, but he is far from melancholy in his manner. He laughs a great deal and his eyes shine with enthusiasm. He is generous in his appreciation of others and spoke glowingly of his friends' qualities; and I think he has a pretty fair opinion of himself too. I do not mean for one second that he is boastful or vain, but he is one of those men who know they have an important role to play and know too that they have the special abilities needed to play it. In this respect such men sound like athletes who speak about their achievements as something separate in a way from themselves—some musicians talk about their ability in the same way. But in spite of his sang-froid Arun is not, or has not been, as calm and unmoved as he likes to appear. It was clear from the way I heard people ask solicitously, 'How are you?' or 'Are you feeling better? You're looking better,' and so on, that the whole episode of being fired and the long battle that went before it had affected him deeply. He now spends his days working at home. Anita said he is very disciplined and works to set hours; once when I came in at about 5.30–6.00 I met him at the door just going out for a run.

When Anita joined us in the sitting room we had omelettes and coffee. It was arranged that I would visit Arun's brother-in-law, the editor of *India Today*, to see if he or his newspaper could help me with my rail ticket. I was not looking forward to another visit to the Central Booking Office.

Suman Dubey kindly looked up all sorts of trains for me but said the paper could really only help with plane tickets. If I flew he'd fix it. But I wanted to go by train, so a visit to the Booking Office was necessary. Suman got me a driver, saying, 'He'll take you and bring you back.'

There were the familiar heaving queues and desperate-looking people hanging around. There was a middle-aged European woman with a little fair-headed girl. The girl was sleeping peacefully with her head on the woman's legs. I queued this time and fixed my reservations quite easily. I met one of the women I'd seen last time and looked for the superintendent whom I had drawn but he was not there. The woman said, 'Oh, hello!' I shook hands with her and asked if I could get a telegram sent to book me a berth from Nagpur to Calcutta. 'Why not?' she said, 'no problem.' She was the woman who'd said she thought London was too crowded.

The driver took me back to the *India Today* office where I met Ajit Ninan, their very good cartoonist. In the open-plan office the Asian Games were on the T.V. and now and then an ironic cheer went up.

I called in to say hello to Romesh but didn't stay long as I'm having dinner at his house tonight with the Shouries.

Outside I did a water-colour of Connaught Place where the Janpath joins it. It's years since I painted directly with water-colour (as opposed to merely colouring a drawing) and I enjoyed it very much. I kept having to gesture to the crowd that formed to not block my view, and the rest of the crowd ticked them off in Hindi, laughing and waving their arms. A beggar woman came up and I gave her a rupee hoping it would send her away. It did.

I did a little shopping and took a scooter-taxi to Jaipur House, the Modern Art Gallery. I wanted to see the pictures by Amrit Shergil, which are extremely good. She was a great painter and had she not died so young (I think she was only twenty-nine), she would undoubtedly have received greater international recognition. However, the best picture in the Gallery was a small water-colour called 'Portrait of a Princess' from the Company Period; mid-19th century, I think. It was an enormously vivacious, sweet and brightly-coloured picture. It was of a pretty girl wearing lots of jewellery with one hand across her breast. Her hair was black and she was framed by a curving blue line against an Indian red background. I did a drawing of her and then went to see whether I could buy a postcard or photo of the painting. I walked into an office where a man was cutting out name tabs for an exhibition of Rodin that is to open tomorrow. Walking into offices seems quite common in India. Anyone seems to be able to wander in anywhere, in rather the same way as at the Red Fort, for example, where there seemed to be nowhere one couldn't go. I don't remember seeing any 'Private: keep out' signs, although I believe part of the Fort is still used as a barracks; nor were there any 'Danger: low wall' or 'Danger: broken balcony' signs when one came across a sheer, stomach-turning drop.

The man in the office was delightful. He stopped what he was

'Portrait of a Princess' from the Company Period

doing to arrange for a photograph to be sent to me since he had no postcards of that picture. I asked him why the picture, which was from some time ago, was included in the Museum of *Modern* Art. He answered that the picture dated from the time European influence first began to show clearly in Indian Art and was therefore of great historical interest.

The way in which Indians stop what they are doing to look after someone, such as me, whom they have met by chance, is one of the most attractive sides of this marvellous country. It may I suppose be related to another side which is delaying and inefficient—the side which never seems quite to get things done on time or finished properly. It may be nothing is ever done quickly because people are forever stopping to enjoy some distracting and interesting experience, or to help someone else in a pleasant and friendly sort of way. I asked the man in the office if I could do a water-colour copy of the little painting. 'Of course,' he said and ordered a chair to be set up for me.

While I was painting, a gang of stony-faced Russians came round with a Russian guide or minder. They took absolutely no notice of me at all, but an art teacher with a gang of little boys all from Bombay stopped and watched. The teacher was another absolute charmer. 'What a lovely line you have,' he said. 'This is my best student,' he said, proudly touching the head of a small boy. I said hello. They stayed watching me until I had finished my drawing and when I had packed up my things they all shook hands with me.

Outside I did a quick water-colour of India Gate. I wanted to go to Hunayan's Tomb, but I was too tired and took a scooter home.

I sat in my room and wrote. After a bit Arun brought me some newspapers from the day his sacking was announced; each had a long front-page account of the event. They were all much the same, all of them very sympathetic to Arun. They saw the whole thing as a tragedy for Indian journalism and a victory for the forces of reaction and oppression. Several carried quotes from individuals who had good reason to dislike Arun but their views clashed with the general bias of pieces.

At about 7.30, Arun, Anita (looking wonderful with a red woollen shawl wrapped closely round her shoulders), and I set off by car for the Thapars' house. The night was chilly, but not freezing cold as Anita insisted it was. Several times when I have mentioned the heat she has expressed amused incredibility. 'You call this *hot*?' The 'armed' guard was patrolling and saluting as we left. Arun and Anita are very fond of him. He first came when they were advised to have a guard; now he is kept on because they can't bear to get rid of him. I asked about his gun: 'Surely it isn't loaded?' They laughed and said they doubted if it would fire even if it was loaded. But it made him feel good. He was an old soldier and felt he should carry a gun, and indeed, it made him look good. Arun said, 'It is a comfort to know he is there.'

At the Thapar house Arun first parked on the broad sidewalk, then changed his mind. Anita explained, 'There are so many car thieves about it is safer inside. All car keys fit all cars, so it's not difficult to steal.'

Romesh's father had collected Indian painting and sculpture and the house is full of treasures. There are stone, wood and bronze sculptures and miniatures from ancient Rajasthan, lovely carpets and wall decorations and little antique objects. Romesh showed me round the house. The work is religious, but it deals with love and the passions in a way Christian Art doesn't. He showed me a picture of a bare-breasted woman sitting on a veranda, her arms raised, her head thrown back.

'She is yearning for Krishna to come to her,' said Romesh, 'and this is how Krishna appears to her.' He pointed to a magnificently-robed figure stepping onto the veranda. A Westerner who does not know the Hindu stories cannot understand the meaning or appreciate the richness of such scenes. Come to that, these days we do not understand much of the symbolism of Christian paintings either. In Indian painting *all* is symbolic. The picture I'd seen in the Jaipur gallery of a woman holding a child aloft I had taken as a picture of just that: a happy and familiar scene executed for the sheer pleasure of it.

However, the keeper had told me it was purely symbolic—though he never got round to telling me its meaning.

The conversation with the Thapars amused me. It concerned the impossibility of getting servants these days.

'They just won't come, and the wages they ask ...'

'... I had to get someone to cut the lawn. Do you know how much?'

(Pause.) Silently mouthed 'Fifteen rupees.'

General gasps of amazement. (Fifteen rupees is about one pound.)

'Excuse me. That is the charge for a day I assume?'

'Yes, a day. Good Lord!' She suddenly saw I could not tell the difference between a day and an hourly rate. Raj is very quick and very sharp. She is witty and laughs often, but she has a shrewd and piercing gaze. I like and respect her very much. There is no nonsense about her, she is frank and blunt and tough. She does not have Romesh's intuitive and romantic side, nor does she show his gentleness and patience; but there is something maternal about her as well. I particularly noted the solicitous way she asked after Arun's health, and at dinner she urged me to have more, once or twice getting up herself to fetch dishes instead of signalling to a silent servant.

The conversation turned to student unrest. This is only similar to Western student unrest in that it is violent. Here it seems to be born out of corruption. Whether or not students get passes or later find jobs depends much more on their contacts and money than on merit. Thus once at university students do not do much work. Those who have plenty of money bully and terrorise other students into joining in strikes or violent action against attempts by the faculty to maintain order. A student assaults a professor. The student is sacked. The other students sit in and demonstrate, disrupting lectures and occupying offices. The faculty, terrified of their university getting a bad name, takes the student back. The screw has turned again. But this activity is not associated at all, as far as I was told, with any familiar student cause such as higher grants, an end to apartheid, anti-government cuts, troops out, free day nurseries and so on. It was another part of the corrupt system, directly related to bad government, the hopeless police and violent law enforcement officers.

Students join riots for professional, rather than political reasons. Romesh said that at one university every student sent down for bad behaviour now works in the government. It was the robber barons again.

I believed these stories completely. They were always prepared to back them up if one expressed doubt, with very convincing arguments and evidence. They are in the business of exposing faults in society since they are journalists whose fame rests on the fact that time and again they have been proved right, and they are jealous of that reputation and careful and methodical. Whether one believes what o ne hears is a complex, mysterious and in the end rather personal matter.

A journalist friend of mine working as a war correspondent in the East developed a technique for detecting whether or not an informant was telling the truth. '. . . It takes a long time—you have to prolong the conversation and ask many questions, and all the time you count how often the informant says "I don't know". If he never says it he is lying. The more often he says it the more likely he is to be telling the truth.'

The food was delicious; the best I've had here. Anita said, 'The food is very very good in Raj's house,' as if to say, 'You are lucky to have this opportunity to try it.' It was served by a silent servant who wore a little cap on his head. Romesh, Raj and Anita ate with their fingers. They picked up the food skilfully and neatly, often in little bits of folded chapatti. I watched fascinated as Raj swept some curry and green peas into a little heap with the tips of her fingers and popped it into her mouth without spilling or splashing a drop. It looked extremely delicate. I wished I could do it but didn't dare try, knowing I would spray the whole table and myself with curry if I did. Raj and Anita did not use the finger bowls that were on the table but left the room to wash their hands when they had finished eating. To someone who has not seen people eating with their fingers like this it may seem absurd to say so, but it is a graceful and delicate habit.

After dinner Romesh teased Arun gently about his yoga exercises. Anita became very lively on the subject: 'Oh! he is so silly, he takes such risks; you know his father was really very worried.' Romesh explained to me, 'You know you can tie yourself in knots and be unable to untie yourself. Even very advanced masters get into difficulty.'

Anita went on: 'He went deaf you know—he made himself deaf; he might have blinded himself. He tried shaking his head.' Cries of disbelief from Raj and Romesh. 'He was standing on his head and he tried shaking it,' said Anita, her eyes wide.

'Why did you do it?' said Romesh shaking his own head and smiling indulgently.

'Boredom,' said Arun faintly, 'I think.' He smiled. 'I'd been standing on my head for a while. I'd tried this position and that. I put my legs open, straight, twisted, and I began thinking to myself, "I wonder if I could shake my head?"' Anita gave a grunt of irritation. 'So I did.' Arun shook his head and smiled. 'Nothing happened. I got up and went to work. On the way to work I noticed a sort of buzzing in my ear, the right ear. By the middle of the day it was quite deaf. I went to the doctor. He scrumpled some paper by my left ear to block any noise and spoke to me. I heard absolutely nothing.'

'What did he do?' asked Romesh, enjoying this story.

'He gave me some pills to increase the circulation of blood in the head. And some cortisone. And one day a little later my hearing came back.'

Romesh laughed and laughed. 'Yoga *and cortisone*—that is the way to health!' he said.

Arun also laughed. 'It was an unpleasant experience,' he said. 'I kept thinking "what if the other ear goes or my eyes?"'

Anita said, 'Ahcha!' as if she couldn't bear to think of it.

Romesh continued to chuckle at his own joke. Raj smiled and shook her head. Arun made as if to go.

'You can't go yet, Arun, sit down,' commanded Raj. 'Wait while I have one more cigarette.' Arun obediently sat down.
'He is exhausted,' murmured Anita.
I wanted the evening to go on and on, but soon after this we went home. Romesh and Raj came out to the car with us into the cool night. Anita wrapped herself tightly in her shawl. The Thapars said to the Shouries, 'We must find time for you to come to the farm, visit the country, it is so relaxing . . .'

There is one more memory I will carry away from the Shouries and that is of their son. He is a beautiful child of about seven or eight; I am not sure of the cause of his condition. He is usually carried in someone's arms, although he has a little wheelchair as well. Several times he joined us while we were sitting around in the Shouries' house. He sat on one of his parents' laps and looked around him and gestured, sometimes staring intently for a few moments at me or at some object that caught his attention. Arun lavished affection on him, kissing him and caressing him lovingly; sometimes lifting him up and playing little games before kissing him again on his cheeks or tummy. I often heard the boy's laughter coming from a room near the kitchen and once saw a servant sitting cross-legged on the floor with the boy. They were looking at each other and the servant was smiling. It was a tender scene. As far as I could tell the boy was never alone or unattended for a second; he always went back quite happily to his young male servant after his parents had to quit their games or go out. There were a number of other people in the house, including Arun's distinguished father, Anita's mother and at least one other servant, sometimes probably more.

Thursday 25th November

I spent the morning after breakfast writing in the sitting room. I had to catch a train at 2.10 and there was not time to do much sightseeing. Also, before the journey I wanted to rest so as not to be too exhausted before I started.

All through the morning Arun had guests; they sat at the other side of the room, talking quietly, giving an impression of planning important business. Arun is a star. The people who came were offering him jobs. In one case a politician was urging him to take a job, any job. 'Your presence is needed. It inhibits people from doing wicked things. They know there is a chance you will find out, sooner or later.'

The servant brought me some lunch and also gave me some food wrapped for the journey, a stuffed paratha and some fruit.

Arun called a taxi and I left Delhi. I count myself very lucky indeed to have met Anita and Arun and I feel very much in their debt. Arun did say about some lickspittle politician, 'A dog with a bone in its mouth cannot bark'; and I suppose anything I have recorded about Arun and his attitudes must be seen in the light of my debt to him. But I do not think my affection for him makes me blind; he is a remarkable man.

Nagpur, Sindi and Gandhi's Ashram

I found my train with some difficulty, my porter being a man of unimaginable stupidity. Several times, I think quite haphazardly, he put down my bags on an empty platform and held out his hand for money. Something told me we had not yet got to the correct place and I'd say, 'Nagpur train' and point. 'Nagpur! Nagpur!' he'd say emphatically and nod his thick skull and hold out his hand. 'Bollocks,' I'd reply and ask someone else. Sure enough we were miles from the right place. I found my train in the end and was pleasantly surprised by how clean and comfortable 'A/C 2-tier' (air-conditioned) travel can be.

The train rapidly filled up with families and assorted travellers. People carried bedrolls and food and drink, as well as luggage. There was a considerable amount of coming and going but not much noise. All was quiet and disorderly; everyone was courteous and patient. A man came with a piece of paper for me to sign stating that I'd found my berth (one of four in the compartment) satisfactorily clean. It was. My only slight concern was that I had been warned by several people to watch my luggage closely because of thieves. I stowed my two bags away and stayed near them.

Once we got under way I sat near my berth by a window. I realised we were taking the same route out of Delhi that I had taken that rainy morning towards Agra. I was on the other side of the train now and could not therefore see the shanty towns and scenes of urban poverty that had so shocked me. I moved to the other side of the train, but found I was worrying about my luggage being out of sight. The only other occupant of this compartment, which on this class of travel is not sealed off from the corridor, was a man of about my age. Once when I got up to check my luggage—a pretty useless precaution because either it was there or gone forever—this man spoke to me.

'Do you have some luggage next door?'

'Yes.'

'Bring it here.'

'But this place may be booked.'

'The conductor will fix it.'

This traveller turned out to be a railwayman himself, an engineer on his way to Nagpur. He was very helpful. His name was O. P. Panchal and he organised the swap-over. Soon I had a window and my luggage together, and relaxed.

The view from the window of the shanty town was nothing like as grim in the hot afternoon sunshine as it had been in the cold wet dawn. The shacks and tents looked far less terrible and the great lakes of filth looked less black and hellish. Mr Panchal explained that we were travelling through an industrial area and that these were the homes of industrial workers. Some jobs provided houses or accommodation for their workers (his did for instance), but some did not and the workers had to fend for themselves. I had thought, quite wrongly, that the people I was looking at were more or less destitute. Not so.

The conductor came and checked my ticket and while he sat by me I watched him deal with several passengers. He was endlessly patient and helpful. One man wanted to change berths and he was instantly given another place. He came back laughing and said, 'There is an M.P. in that one; we'd better leave him there.' The conductor also chuckled and explained it must have been a last-minute requisition. Soon, the M.P. arrived and politely explained the situation. Another place was found. A man arrived looking harassed. 'Did you give me back my rail pass?'

'Of course, sir, why should I keep it?' It turned out the man had given it to his servant on the station instead of some other document. This problem was also dealt with.

The next problem was brought by a woman. 'I have a ticket

but no reservation,' she said, 'and I have a small kid with me.' She did too, a very noisy, pretty little brat of about five.

'All right, Madam. Please do not worry. Everyone will help you,' said the conductor. All this time he was filling out endless forms, and later in the journey I saw him still at it, a huge ledger open on his knee.

Mr Panchal was curious about me and my work and family. He told me he had already married off one of his daughters, who now had a son. He smiled proudly when I congratulated him. He now wants to marry off one of his sons, then his younger, seventeen-year-old daughter and finally the youngest son. Then he and his wife would like to do some travelling.

The city gave way to the country, looking just as full of activity. In the villages and in the fields scores of people toiled, talked in groups, and walked. There were also monkeys and exotic birds. I saw some tall grey birds with red heads, herons or cranes perhaps, and various smaller species including pretty green parrots flapping madly from tree to tree.

We passed through some desert where Mr Panchal explained dacoits lived. He told me they came from the local community and that 'society often forces them to become dacoits.'

'How?' I asked.

'Suppose a young soldier comes home on leave,' he said. 'He finds his family is having a row with some neighbours. Naturally he joins in on his family's side. He shows his revolver and says "I am a military man", and maybe he shoots someone! Well, he has to become a dacoit. He runs away otherwise the police come and take him.' It seemed to me slightly unfair to blame society for this sorry tale but I did not say so.

'And do the dacoits live out there?' I asked gesturing towards the strange landscape of escarpments and gullies, and dry rocky wasteland.

'Yes, out there, lots of them!'

'Do they live alone? Do they have women with them?'

He slightly misunderstood my question. 'No, not many women dacoits. One woman has organised her gang. One woman dacoit. She is well known but they haven't caught her yet.'

'Do they rob the local people?'

'No, they do not harm ordinary local people. Every village has a money lender or a landowner who has many rupees. They rob them.'

'And do they rob travellers? People on trains and buses?'

'Oh yes, very often,' he said, as the train slowly came to a halt. 'That is why every train carries four armed guards. At least four armed guards.' I'd seen them around. They do not inspire confidence; they look half-asleep and carry ancient 303s. Mr Panchal looked out at the desolate countryside.

'Good hideout,' he said, 'for dacoits.'

'Are they well armed, the dacoits?'

'Very well armed: sten guns, machine guns, hand grenades. It is easy to get guns in India.'

I was thinking how incredibly fed up I'd be to have to hand over my watch, signet ring and wallet to some bloody dacoit. I wondered if it came to it whether I could hide them. I could imagine some wily robber looking at the pale marks on my wrist and third finger. In my imagination I saw him waving a sten gun and saying 'O.K. Where are they?'

'Why have we stopped?' I asked extremely casually.

'Oh, some hold up,' he said.

After a few moments a train thundered past the window and we got under way again.

I ate some of Arun's food. It was very good and very welcome. When it grew dark I inflated the pillow Richard had advised me to buy and lay down. I was comfortable and knew Mr Panchal would wake me at Nagpur. I slept well.

We arrived at Nagpur at five in the morning. I had some difficulty with taxi drivers and rickshaws. They clamoured at me, demanding very high rates, and I had no idea of where to go. The girl in the travel agency at the Oberoi, New Delhi, had suggested Jagson's Hotel. I asked a cycle rickshaw, 'How much to Jagson's Hotel?'

'Ten rupee.'

A young man passing by said, 'Don't pay him more than one-fifty or two. That is the correct rate.'

'Thank you,' I said, and to the rickshaw boy, 'five rupees.' I held up one hand, fingers spread.

'O.K.,' he said, and we set off. It was dark and once we had left the station the streets were empty. After about two hundred yards the boy stopped and dismounted.

'Ten rupee,' he said.

'Five,' I said.

'Ten.'

Angrily I said, 'Five—are you going to stop right here?'

Hurriedly, perhaps alarmed by my ferocity, he remounted. 'Jagson Hotel,' he said.

He stopped at a sign saying 'Blue Moon Hotel'.

'This very good hotel,' he said. I'd heard of it, so I went in. It was full. We went on. He stopped at another hotel. 'Very good hotel,' he said. I looked inside. Yes, they had a room but it was awful with a great air conditioning machine hissing and wheezing just outside the door.

'Too noisy,' I said. We headed towards yet another hotel. 'Jagson's Hotel now!' I ordered.

'This very good hotel. . . .'

'Jagson's,' I said firmly; and that's where he went, rather ill-humouredly.

I booked a room. The first one they showed me was too small; the second was fine. I went outside to pay my rickshaw boy. I gave him a five and added a two to shut him up.

'Ten,' he insisted, raising his hands and refusing to take the money.

'Seven.'

'Ten.'

'Oh, forget it then,' I said and went inside to check in.

'Sir! Sir!' he called.

Inside I explained to the desk clerk about my problem with the boy. The clerk said five was generous. I gave the seven to someone standing by saying, 'Here, you pay him.' He disappeared and I noticed he put the two in his pocket. In a moment he came back and returned my two-rupee note.

I lay down and dozed until about 8.30.

Friday 26th November

Jagson's Hotel is nothing like as luxurious as the hotels I have become used to in India. That is not to say that it's not perfectly clean and comfortable with good service and a pleasant restaurant; but it is in a fairly shabby little street (not shabby by Nagpur standards, I was to find out) and it is pretty basic. This suits me very well. I've discovered that very grand hotels upset me a bit. They feel like a good thing for about forty-eight hours, but after that may begin to do a certain sort of harm. I'm not sure I could sustain this argument for very long and there are times in life when to be a guest in a luxury hotel is the most desirable thing in the world, but their world has nothing to do with real life and one can begin to suffer, almost without knowing it, from withdrawal symptoms. Extremely good professional service is a heartless thing. Boiled right down to its essence, perhaps what I am saying is that luxury hotels remove one too far not only from life's difficulties, which is why you are there in the first place, but also life's ordinary pleasures.

Anyway I got up, had breakfast and almost without planning it hired a car for the day to visit Sindi, Wardha and Gandhi's Ashram. When I read in books or articles 'I hired a car', I often get irritated. I want to know *how* did you hire the bloody thing? How did you *know* how to? Did you lie down in the street and drum your heels until they brought you a car? The answer is that hotels in India, and all over the world probably, will offer you a car almost as soon as you arrive. In this case I asked the reception clerk and he directed me to the hotel travel agent directly across the little road. My driver, who took a young companion along with us, spoke no English. He was very small and slim with a sparse beard and long oiled hair. He was expressionless and even sinister, although his young friend was amiable enough.

I went at first to the railway station and reserved my berth to Calcutta on Monday. Then we drove through the crowded streets out of Nagpur and down the straight high road for Wardha, which is about eighty kilometres away. Indians drive in the same weird way wherever I have been. The fundamental attitude is 'If I'm bigger than you, get out of my way'. One variation on this is 'If we are the same size, may the best man win'. Traffic lights, intersections, blind corners, and hazards like these don't count; they are ignored; and which side of the road to use is also optional for extended, heart-stopping periods.

All drivers sound their horns more or less permanently, even when the person they are blasting at is obviously in as much of a hurry as they are. Once we stopped at a level crossing. There were several cars waiting each side. The barrier was down and a train obviously due any second. Nevertheless my driver leaned ritually on the horn for several seconds. Once the train had passed and the crossing keeper was resetting his signals and clearly about to raise the barrier—*honk honk honk*! No one takes any more notice of car horns than they do of anything else.

One mitigating factor is that all vehicles are in terrible condition. While this means brakes and steering are dodgy, high speed and quick acceleration are equally impossible. The other thing that makes this system work after a fashion is the personality of the driver, or rather their attitude to one another. The European style of driving with insults and abuse hurled from one speeding, dicing, cutting-in machine to another does not seem to be part of India's way. No flashing headlights, no V-signs, no sign of anger at all. The worst I've witnessed is a muttered remark to a pedestrian or cyclist who has been slower than usual in getting out of the way. This is always received with a bland stare. In the midst of what seems to be utter chaos, the individual Indians remain calm and relaxed. One acquires some confidence from this after a bit—not a lot, but some.

The high road to Wardha is not wide; a lorry and a car cannot pass each other comfortably, and it is very crowded, but not only with cars or lorries.

Before I came to India a friend asked me, 'What are you going to see?' He meant what was I going to look for. I said I was not sure, apart of course from the Taj, maybe, or the Red Fort, but that I'd know what I wanted to see when I saw it. After a few miles of driving down this road I suddenly realised, 'Of course, *this* is it, this is what I came for.' Somewhere in my mind, probably from the description of the great trunk road in *Kim*, I have carried for years the picture of a crowded, hot, long, dusty Indian road and I have always wanted to see one. Funnily enough I didn't even think of that for at least fifteen or twenty minutes driving but then, instead of looking excitedly from one exotic detail to another, I suddenly saw it as a whole and realised that this was 'it'.

There were straggling groups of women and children walking the verges, some carrying loads on their heads; numerous herds of cattle and goats that the cars and lorries and battered buses threaded their way through, honking and patient; stalls selling food and fruit under the shade of trees and people resting, squatting on their heels; cyclists and motor-bikes wobbling along and the people wearing an incredible variety of costume. There were children driving individual cows, there were bullock carts and road menders, and all were crowded together, all jostling for space; yet all was very peaceful and purposeful.

To a European, bored with everything at home looking the same, tasting the same, costing the same from Portugal to Vienna, this sight was as refreshing and wonderful as anything I could imagine. It was one of those times when one thinks 'I must come back here', before one has even completed the experience. This is something I've often chided one of my children for doing. 'Just enjoy it now—don't think about coming back for more.' How often we tick off our children for doing what we ourselves do all the time.

I revelled in this drive; it never grew tedious. I never minded the jolts or the heat. It was sheer delight. The fields that bordered the road were also busy: farmers ploughed and tilled, and people walked to and fro. I saw thin old ladies carrying huge loads on their heads looking like duchesses practising advanced deportment exercises.

This was a scene into which words like poverty and hardship were difficult to fit. Certainly the people, or many of them, are poor and I have no doubt their lives are hard, but being there and seeing them, at least for me this first time, I found I could not hold on to such complicated and serious notions. I gazed unthinking, simply glad to be there.

As I write memories crowd back into my mind. I noticed a group of boys throwing stones, and thought how unusual it is in India to see anyone making an unnecessary or useless effort. Then I saw they were bombarding some large monkeys who were in a field damaging some crop that I did not recognise. There were many birds in the fields and the inevitable buzzards or kites wheeled through the sky.

After about an hour's drive we turned off the main road onto a smaller dustier version, sometimes little more than a track. This was less populated and even the fields seemed suddenly emptier. On and on we went through the heat and the dust, the driver grim and expressionless, his companion silent and preoccupied. Where on earth was I going? (With a thrill of horror a headline flashed before me: 'Mystery of cartoonist's whereabouts baffles police'.) We crossed a railway and at last arrived in a large sprawling village or town. This was nothing like anything else I'd seen before. The streets were unmetalled, the buildings low and mostly whitewashed brick or mud. Lined up along the approaches to the town were scores of wagons, each loaded with a large bale, and the whole place as usual was very, very crowded. This rural crowd was slightly different from the urban scenes I have become used to. It was dusty rather than dirty and there were innumerable children, pigs, goats and cattle mingling with the crowd, and a few dogs. There were almost no motor vehicles; I noticed only two rather official-looking vans.

Before I left London I had asked an Indian friend, Kranti Nandanwar, where I should go in India. Everyone else had said

Delhi, Simla, Calcutta, Kashmir, and most often, Rajasthan. Kranti had said, 'The Deccan. Go to Nagpur in Central India. India is changing, but there it is changing slower than anywhere else. There you will get an idea of an older India.' She went on to give me the addresses and names of some relatives who live near Nagpur, particularly that of her mother who is staying in Sindi for a few months waiting for her daughter-in-law to get a visa for England. I had instantly resolved to take Kranti's advice, and that was why I now stood on the edge of Sindi, wondering what to do next.

The address was Ward 7 Sindi, the Sindi equivalent of saying N.W.10 London. 'It could be a big place,' the travel agent in Nagpur had said. My driver made a few enquiries and led me across an open space towards a crumbling but vaguely official-looking building behind a rusty wire fence. (It used to be a hospital and was now a dispensary.)

The old hospital, Sindi

Inside we met a very, very sleepy, chubby young man, slightly resembling Benny Hill. He gestured to me to sit down and spoke in Hindi with the driver. His English was not terrific and his accent very thick, but in his sleepy way he seemed prepared to help. 'Mrs Nandanwar—here—three months—now—maybe here—maybe not here,' he said slowly, not moving his lips and apparently only just able to keep his eyes open. His face assumed the ghost of a smile. I said eagerly, 'Can we go and look for her?' He raised a fat arm and let it drop again. We sat there. I think he may have been expecting more of this stimulating conversation but perhaps he was just rallying himself for the journey. Eventually he stood up and we went outside into the heat. We got into the car and he directed the driver through the narrow streets. I was offended by the driver honking just as loudly in this quiet place as he did in Nagpur. Honking is a chronic affliction in India.

I chatted with my new guide. It turned out he was a doctor. He had trained not far away and had now been posted to Sindi, where he was happy. There were five other doctors in Sindi but he was the only State Doctor; the others were all private. 'Your services are free then?' I asked. His eyes turned slowly towards me and like a dummy owned by a drugged ventriloquist he uttered the word, 'Yes.' Conversation with him was possible once you got used to the tempo, if tempo is the right word, and he was very friendly.

After a bit we stopped because the car could go no further. The doctor and I went first to a shop where a man indicated that I should sit next to him on a padded bench. This gentleman, who did not speak English, turned out to be one of Kranti's 'uncles', Mr Bokade. She had told me she used the word 'uncle' to indicate 'older male relative', however distant. He was very gracious and welcoming and we chatted, using the doctor as a translator. Several other people gathered round and listened and joined in.

It is very difficult to convey the atmosphere of this sort of meeting. It is in a way very formal; you wish fervently not to offend or do or say anything wrong. I felt as if I was among aristocrats, whose perfect manners and graceful movements made me feel clumsy and uncertain. And yet the atmosphere was so cordial and friendly that at the same time I felt included and welcomed in a peculiarly charming way.

Sindi

The doctor had now discovered Mrs Nandanwar's address and we walked on another quarter of a mile, crossing a stream on the way where women were washing clothes and some children were flying kites. Several sleek horses grazed on the banks of the stream. At last we stopped at a house and stepped onto the porch. I noticed that the doctor did not remove his sandals, so I didn't remove my shoes. Kranti had told me not to worry about etiquette apart from taking off my shoes if I were to enter a house. Perhaps the porch didn't count. After a few moments a distinguished-looking woman appeared, wearing a yellow sari. She looked surprised and curious to see me. She spoke English fluently.

‘Are you Mrs Nandanwar, Kranti’s mother?’

‘Yes I am.’

‘My name is Nick Garland. I am a friend of Kranti’s. Did she tell you I might visit you?’

‘No, I have not heard from her for four months.’

I explained how I came to be here and what I was doing in India. She asked me to sit down and apologised for her manner; she’d been in bed for a couple of days with fever and a sore throat. I said I was very sorry to hear it—perhaps I should go and disturb her no longer, but she waved to me to sit down and said that aspirins had made her feel better.

‘Perhaps you should consult the doctor,’ I said indicating the sleepwalker beside me. She laughed and said her doctor had already been a great help. My doctor smiled lazily.

At first conversation was a little stilted and she seemed as shy as I felt, but as we became used to each other everything grew easier.

Tea was brought and a man joined us, but was not introduced. A woman sat half-hidden, watching us through an open door. A beautiful little girl of six or seven flitted about, running away every time I looked at her, and a boy slightly older leaned on a door post listening shyly. Outside, now and then, someone walked by in the white sunshine.

I had asked Kranti if she thought anyone would mind if I did some drawing in her uncle's home. She said she thought not but would rather I did not draw her mother. I asked Mrs Nandanwar if she would object if I drew the porch we were sitting on.

'It is not my house,' she replied. 'I will enquire.' She got up and went to speak to the woman, who was watching us from another room. 'It's all right, you may draw the porch,' she said. After I had done a quick sketch, which I thought would be a present for Kranti in return for her help, I began to draw the little girl who was standing watching me. Her name is Manisha. She fled as soon as she realised what I was doing. The man ordered her back and obediently she returned, standing in agonised embarrassment until I had finished; though she was quite interested in the result.

By now Mrs Nandanwar was quite relaxed. She invited me to dinner either tonight or Sunday. Tonight was difficult; I had much else to do. Also I had not slept much the night before and would be dropping with fatigue later. We agreed on Sunday, always supposing I could get a car that would wait for me, so that I could get back to my hotel.

I was offered some betel and tried chewing it. It was tasteless and hard. Mrs Nandanwar laughed and said it should be chewed with the leaf and something else and that then it made the mouth all red. I said I had noticed that.

Manisha Bokade

Boys in Sindi

On my way back to the car I stopped and did several drawings, much to the delight of some children who gathered to watch each time I opened my book.

The doctor conducted me back to Mr Bokade's shop where I had sat earlier. Again I was asked to sit down and have tea. Again I felt welcomed and comfortable. I was offered more betel and some seeds. I took a seed and chewed it. It was very strong and not unpleasant. It may have been a cardamom seed. I drank my tea and did a drawing of some boys who had gathered to stare at me with large dark eyes.

I was a little worried about my driver and his companion . . . *(I am writing this on the porch of Jagson's Hotel on Saturday morning. A handsome brown rat has just crossed the porch near my feet and is now sitting in the shade a couple of yards away by a window. A man noticed my look of surprise when I saw the rat and he burst out laughing. No one else has taken or is taking the slightest notice of it.)*

. . . who had been waiting all this time. It was now about 1.30–2.00. I asked the doctor to give them a ten-rupee note that I handed him to buy themselves something to eat and drink. He came back soon saying they preferred to wait until we got to Wardha before they ate.

After finishing my tea, I got back into the car. We dropped the doctor at his surgery. He said he would probably not be around on Sunday so I said farewell to him and thanked him earnestly for his kindness and help. He nodded and smiled, raising a hand with a gigantic effort to cut off my thanks.

We had barely regained the main road when the car began making an awful noise and smoke began to drift from the engine. The driver grimaced and continued for a bit but soon pulled up. He got out and opened the bonnet. Smoke and steam rose in billowing clouds. The radiator was empty. He took off the oil cap and blue smoke emerged. Calmly he closed it again and said to me, 'Water.'

'And how,' I replied. He looked down the dusty road and tossed his head, meaning, 'O.K., let's go.' 'He can't be going to drive on,' I thought, but he did until we reached a road-mending gang, some of whom were eating, while others sat around on a heap of gravel. A woman brought a can of water from somewhere and it was sloshed into the radiator and over the engine. It seemed to do the trick, because for the rest of the day we had no trouble.

Breakdown on the road to Wardha

The drive to Gandhi's Ashram at Savagram took some time and it turned out to be exactly what I expected. The place had a strangely familiar sort of atmosphere that I didn't at first identify. The Ashram consists of a number of simple low mud huts each bearing a sign in English and Hindi describing how or when Gandhi or one of his followers had had it built and for what purpose it was designed. Gravelled walks take you from place to place and one or two groups of visitors were wandering around. Some of the buildings were occupied by people resting or reading or spinning. The place is evidently lived in and alive; it is not just a shrine.

Gandhi's Ashram, Savagram

Inside most of the small mud-built houses were odd-looking designs modelled on the walls with an art nouveau look to them: simple curving shapes, sometimes abstract, sometimes resembling trees or perhaps flowers. I asked whether Gandhi had designed them and an elderly man who had been spinning said no, they had been designed by a European woman, a devoted follower of Gandhi's.

These designs suddenly identified the atmosphere for me. As a child, I had attended a Rudolf Steiner school for some years. That school had the same air of purity and goodness, the same dusty simplicity and complete absence of any kind of show or violence, giving visitors the same warm, uncomplicated welcome. In fact although I wrote uncomplicated there is one slight complication, but it is so elusive and difficult to describe I may not be able to convey it. Both the Rudolf Steiner school and the Gandhi Ashram have a faint but unmistakeable proselytising element, that reaches out for you from an apparent or assumed passivity. You are in fact being preached at. They want, if they can, though only by example, to change you to their way of thinking.

The man I had asked about the designs led me into a hut and sat down. I also sat down and he motioned to five or six other visitors who followed us to sit too. He gave us a short talk on Gandhi and answered questions. He was a vigorous grey-haired man of uncertain age. He could have been seventy. He was wearing a simple white cotton *dhoti*. Before I left him he said, 'Our strength comes from the good simple lives we lead.' I laughed and said that he was an excellent testimony to the merits of the system. He laughed too.

He showed me a telephone that the British had had installed so that Gandhi could confer with the Governor General.

'Bapu was so grateful,' said the guide and he laughed again. 'We were fighting the British and yet they were so *kind*: they gave us the telephone.' It was a sort of compliment to me, I thought. 'It was a hot line,' he said. The modern expression jarred unexpectedly in this other-worldly place.

Later, as I took a last look round after doing a couple of drawings, I passed a guest house and as I did the guide walked near me. 'That is our guest house,' he said. 'You are always welcome there.'

What relevance all this has to modern India and its problems, I have absolutely no idea. I came away with the glimmering of an understanding of what a gigantic personality and man Gandhi had been and the faintest impression that all this, whilst having a kind of nobility deriving from its powerful simplicity, could no longer help or guide India forward today.

By now the afternoon was getting cooler and the shadows lengthened. I wanted a drink and a rest. The drive home was long and bumpy. We stopped once for tea at a wayside place where both my companions ate and drank. I did not relish drinking even the tea, which came in a fearful-looking glass. On the other hand to leave it untouched seemed very rude after the driver had politely ordered it for me. Even more unwilling to hurt his feelings than to damage my own digestion I tried surreptitiously dropping a water-purifying tablet into the glass. This produced an unexpectedly dramatic chemical reaction. Pale yellow foam rose hissing and bubbling from the tea. I tried to convey the impression that everything was under control in case anyone had noticed and took out my sketch book, ignoring the volcanic drink, most of which was soon flowing lazily over the dirty table top. Luckily people took no notice of me and I sat alone drawing and resting, enjoying looking at the scene and the flowing traffic on the road.

Outside Nagpur

Saturday 27th November

Travelling alone is a new experience for me. There is one great advantage to being by yourself. You are completely your own master. If you want to stop, you stop. If you want to move, you move. You eat and drink just when you feel you want to and I think there must be those who get addicted to this state of affairs. The sense of freedom is exhilarating. But a feeling of loneliness can overcome me and be very oppressive. I quickly develop a need for companions and the support of friends. I want to feel protected and miss my family very much. I desperately want someone familiar to talk to and the chance to relate my adventures to my friends. My journal and drawings help but it is not the same as talking. (I think this explains to a certain degree my strong feelings for Arun, Anita, Romesh and Raj, whom I felt became friends.) I suppose that experienced travellers learn to cope with this problem, but I have not mastered it. My personality is not really cut out for such isolation. I find sleeping difficult and have several times taken sleeping pills at night to blot out the emptiness of my hotel room. At times one can feel a little mad. I do not want to exaggerate this sensation, but it forms an important part of this journey and I feel I should note it down. I spent the whole of the morning and much of the afternoon writing. I sat on the porch outside the hotel moving my table each time the sun moved round to where I was sitting. It was uncomfortably hot out of the shade. I drank coffee and lime juice and watched the passers-by.

A young Sikh came and introduced himself to me and urged me to visit Bombay, to come to his home and meet his family. He insisted I came down the road to see a photograph of a Sikh temple. Actually he wanted to introduce me to his brother-in-law (or his cousin, I couldn't tell which) in whose office the photo was. The neat and tidy office was over a garage or workshop of some sort where several young men tinkered with unbelievably battered small motor-bikes, none of which looked as if it would ever go again. The elegant young brother-in-law ordered tea and asked questions about my work and reasons for visiting India.

'Let us talk frankly,' he said. 'Now—should India have spent so much money on the Asian Games? Has it been worth it?'

I said it would be a long time before its value could be assessed. It depended on how well it all worked and whether or not India's international prestige was so increased that they would eventually be awarded the honour of hosting the 1992 Olympiad. 'I imagine that this is the great prize for Mrs Gandhi,' I said, as if I knew. He began to reel off statistics about India's productivity, progress and independence. I got a feeling he was pretty conservative. When I tactfully suggested that the government might sometimes deal violently with opposition, or corruptly in managing its affairs, he allowed that this could in certain circumstances be true, but India was very large, very backward in places and if such things happened then sooner or later it would 'come out' and the culprits would be punished.

He had visited England some years ago. He had made an enormously long trip by motor-bike, staying in youth hostels with three companions. They had driven there and back I gathered, and had taken six months over it. In Britain, which he had liked very much, he visited London, Wales and Scotland. He knew very little about our country though and could name no politicians except Mrs Thatcher. He was extremely courteous and obviously quite affluent, referring to himself at one point as 'a man in my position ...'

He told me about his interest in guns and hunting. He belongs to some sort of group or club who illegally shoot deer, buffalo, sambuck and other game, some to eat, some just for the sport. He owns three guns: a shotgun, a 30.06 Springfield rifle and a 470 double-barrelled rifle, a John Rigby. 'We do it,' he said, 'in order to keep our weapons in order, and ourselves in order, and for the adventure.'

'Tell me,' I asked, 'is it illegal to own the guns, or just to hunt the animals?'

'Oh, just to kill the animals,' he said. 'The other members of the group are not all Sikhs. There are Moslems, and two Christians. There is nothing political about the gang at all ... it is a hunting group.'

He also owns a Webley & Scott .32 six-shot revolver. 'That is for my personal protection.'

'Why do you need protection?'

'If I am carrying a lot of money or travelling by road some distance I like to carry my hand gun.'

'Where do you carry it? On your hips? Under your arm?'

'If I am in my car, here,' he said, patting his armpit. 'Because I like to be able to draw it quickly.' He made a fumbling gesture by his hip to show that it was difficult to draw from there when sitting down. 'But if I am walking, here,' and he patted his hip.

'Is it unusual for people to carry hand guns in this country?'

'Yes.'

The other Sikh showed no interest at all in this subject. Indeed when I asked him about it he expressed mild contempt.

'It is very dangerous to hunt tiger,' said the John Wayne man.

'Are there tigers round here?'

'Oh yes, but it is dangerous. You can get fifteen years for killing a tiger!'

'Have you ever drawn your revolver in your own defence?' I pressed him.

'I would much rather not use my gun,' he said emphatically. 'It takes so long explaining everything to the police. So many questions arise . . .' he said vaguely.

I was very glad to hear it, but said nothing.

'But I would not hesitate to use it, not for a second, if I had to,' he said, prepared to overcome any amount of red tape if the need arose.

Somehow or other we got onto the subject of coal miners. There is a good deal of coal mining around here. He said, 'They are very highly paid,' and explained they could earn more than an educated man, or a bank manager for instance, even though they could not even sign their names. 'They just make a mark with the thumb,' he said, sneering. I had read in the papers about the appalling death-toll among miners from various chest diseases.

'They ruin their health,' I said.

He allowed that they ruined their health and that many died. 'But,' he insisted, 'they are very highly paid.'

Another subject that cropped up was racialism. He told me, and others have said the same thing, that stories of racial trouble in England anger and horrify Indians and it tends to turn them towards other countries for trade, or cultural and sporting exchanges. 'Mind you, we have our own racial troubles. There are a great many niggers here. They come to study mostly and they are not popular.'

'Excuse me—did you say *niggers*?' I asked.

'Yes, niggers—from Uganda, Kenya, everywhere.' He suddenly realised why I had asked and smiled broadly. 'We will not use the slang *niggers*: negroes,' he corrected.

He offered to take me hunting that night. 'We leave at about eight thirty or nine and return three or four in the morning. You will have to bring some warm clothes—it gets cold. I will show you what we get up to.'

I was very much in two minds about this. It seemed feeble to turn down the offer; on the other hand I had no idea at all what I would be letting myself in for. I hedged. 'Think it over,' he said coolly. 'I'll ring you later.' He asked where I was staying.

I thought it over hard for the rest of the day and found it very difficult to know what to do. I was not fantastically keen on a sixty-kilometre drive in the dead of night with these unknown cowboys, even less keen because it was illegal. I've seen armed Indian police and they scare me. On the other hand, could I turn down such an adventure without admitting, to myself at least, that I'm a yellow-bellied coward? Actually I know I'm a coward already, so that wasn't the problem.

I went for a walk round the town. I looked at musty little stalls and bought odds and ends. There is absolutely nothing touristy about Nagpur. Every second shop was a mechanical-repair shop of some sort. Thousands of motor-bikes were being attended to.

Boys, Nagpur

When I stopped to draw in the back streets I attracted an enormous crowd of shrieking, giggling children; some of them begged me to draw them, and posed, mugging for me. I drew them and when I showed them the drawings they became beside themselves with excitement, grabbing at my precious notebooks and screaming with delight.

The streets are poor with occasional brightly-coloured temples. Goats and other livestock wander round apparently untended.

I became overcome with an attack of the blues. I wanted to get out of the place. I cursed the Sikh and felt bad.

Back in my hotel I sent out for some shampoo. The pretty girl smiled. 'What sort?' she said.

'The best—the sort you use.'

She laughed.

I washed and lay on my bed reading. When the Sikh rang I told him I wasn't coming. The disappointment in his voice made me feel awful. I explained I was just plain nervous. He had told me it was illegal. I was in a foreign country and felt uncertain about the whole thing. I thanked him very much and hoped he'd understand.

'We've never had any trouble,' he said mournfully, 'yet.' He said he'd try to visit me tomorrow.

I hung up feeling utterly pathetic and furious with myself. But it was too late.

I felt lousy for the rest of the evening, and in the end took a sleeping pill.

Sunday 28th November

I spent most of the morning writing on the hotel porch. The air was so filthy that I had to keep blowing gritty dust off the page and anything that was left standing instantly became covered with a layer of dirt.

I arranged for a car to take me to Sindi in the afternoon and sent out for some sweets to take as a present for Mrs Nandanwar and Mr Bokade's children. The sweets came beautifully wrapped up in a promisingly heavy parcel. The boy who had fetched them said, 'They have come from the most famous sweet shop in Nagpur!' As soon as I was in the car, with the same driver, who was very smiley and friendly today, I suppose because he now knew me a little and because I had tipped him generously, my spirits rose. The road was not quite as full as it had been on Friday but just as entertaining. I noticed a dead dog still lying just where it had been two days ago. The horrible stench of rotting dog filled the car for a second or two as we passed it. It mildly surprised me that no one had budged it, but then if I'd been passing a dead fox at home I certainly wouldn't have touched it.

I had come to Sindi early in the afternoon, so that I could look around and do some drawing before dinner, but first I went to Mr Bokade's house to let Mrs Nandanwar know that I was here. She was very welcoming. We had tea. Several men arrived and sat, unintroduced, on the porch with us. I gave her the parcel of sweets for which she thanked me before carrying it away. After a bit Mr Bokade arrived. He is in his sixties, I would guess, and was wearing a *dhoti*. He had a gentle manner and spoke very good English. He had lived in England for about six years during the fifties. He spent some time in hospital in England and while there had taken up painting. He showed me five or six of his pictures. They were done from photographs in oil paint and were all portraits. There was Churchill, Gaitskell, Mr Bokade's father and Prince Charles. They were very accomplished and ambitious paintings. Churchill was posed against a background of dark red rhododendrons and large green leaves. I asked if he had maintained his interest in painting but he said no. When the pictures had been hung in a restaurant his brother-in-law had owned in London, people used to ask to buy them but he'd always refused. 'I told them I did them purely for my own pleasure, not to sell.' Eventually he had returned to India with his pictures and soon recovered his health. He now felt very content to live in Sindi. Manisha was his youngest child.

'Now,' said Mrs Nandanwar, 'what do you want to do?'

'I'd like to walk around the village and perhaps do some drawings,' I told her. 'That is why I have arrived for dinner so early.' Mr Bokade said he would like to come too.

We wandered through the village and I asked him about everything we saw. Why were the walls of many houses covered in straw matting? That was to protect the mud walls from being washed away by the rain. What are these people doing? 'They are preparing cotton to be taken to a loom where it will be woven. I'll show you.' 'Why is that building decorated like that? Is it a temple of some sort?' 'No—that is someone's house. He has just painted it like that.'

Sindi

When I stopped to draw, children came running over to watch. Sometimes Mr Bokade chided them gently, telling them to stop jogging my arm or to stop standing right in front of me on tiptoe and trying to look at my work.

I asked him if Sindi had changed during his lifetime; he was born here. At first he said no, and smiled at the idea of this place ever changing. He somehow conveyed the comment that the place hadn't really ever changed, not for hundreds and hundreds of years. Wagons had always been pulled by bullocks and cotton woven on that sort of loom and houses constructed of that mud; these things did not change. Neither did the gods worshipped in the temples nor the crops grown in the fields. But after a few moments he begun to describe considerable changes. The population had fallen during his lifetime. It had been ten to fifteen thousand when he was a boy and now it was something less than nine thousand. The reason is that people leave to work in the towns and factories because there they can get more money. It means it is getting harder to find farm workers. He now does things himself on his farm that used always to be done by hired labour. He said the way the orange crop was sold had altered. It used to be sold to businessmen in large quantities while the oranges were still 'small' (I think he might have meant unripe). The businessmen shipped them far away to distant markets in baskets that were made in the village. This now no longer happened. The businessmen now buy 'big' oranges elsewhere, so the farmers have to sell their own produce in local markets. This has meant that the basket makers are not needed and that craft has died out.

In the centre of Sindi is a sort of market place or open area where there are a number of little stalls. I saw a man selling little clay figures looking like crude rabbits or horned beasts. I asked what they were. Mr Bokade said dismissively, 'They are

Sindi

nothing, silly things. Simple people buy them because they think they have the power to cure illness. When the illness has gone they put these things in the temple.' I said I wanted to buy one. Mr Bokade said, 'No, no, it's nonsense.' 'But do you mind if I buy one?' I asked, thinking he might be offended for some reason that I couldn't fathom. He said, 'No, I don't mind.' I picked up one of the little objects and asked, 'How much?' The stall owner said something and several children translated 'twenty-five paise'. I handed over a coin and put the clay creature in my pocket. All the children burst out laughing.

As we walked through the streets of the rambling, sprawling place I asked whether the streets are named. 'No, only that place,' he said, pointing to an open area and saying its name. 'How does the postman find people's houses then?' I asked. The answer was that the village is divided up into wards and I suppose that is enough. Everyone in any given ward will know their neighbours and thus people can be found.

Evening was falling and people lit fires and candles. The still air was smoky and the scene became more and more pretty. Cows and goats and chickens moved through the streets which remained full of people. All the houses were open and everywhere people sat and talked or strolled about or worked. It was a busy, cheerful place, crowded but not noisy. Even the children seemed to run about and play without making much sound. Perhaps the noise just floated away into the huge empty dark sky.

We seemed to be heading somewhere, for Mr Bokade continued at a leisurely pace out of the village towards a cluster of larger buildings in the direction of the main road. I asked him where we were going.

'To the ginning factory,' he replied.

We approached a fenced-off factory, consisting of two or three lit-up sheds before which were huge piles of roughly-baled raw cotton, and a vast white mountain of unbaled cotton from which men and women were carrying loads into one of the sheds. A continuous chain of figures walked to and fro endlessly, although the white mountain never grew smaller. Mr

Bokade at first said we couldn't go in, but then seemed to arrange for us to enter, because we were beckoned forward.

Cotton gin, Sindi

A man accompanied us first to a shed where cotton that had been cleaned of impurities was being pressed and properly baled for transportation elsewhere. In this shed were two gigantic cast-iron presses worked by many men and boys. It was dark inside and the clatter of the hydraulic machinery was very loud. The work was heavy but conducted at a fairly slow steady pace. As we entered, a load of cotton which had been pressed one way was being swung across to a second machine to be pressed again and sewn into a sacking bale. As the great black machine exerted its inhuman strength the cotton creaked and groaned in its grip. In bold letters on the front of the press were the words 'HENRY BERRY & CO LTD LEEDS'. Its sister machine was dated 1888. It was a piece of pure Victorian England, still alive and healthy and working; an astonishing sight and most unexpected. I watched the engineers working the hydraulic machinery: great shiny steel pistons with polished brass plates and iron bolts, all dripping with oil and sluicing with water, pounded and rose and fell making a tremendous noise. Henry Berry would have been proud, although no doubt not surprised, to see his creation still going strong.

Part of cotton press, Sindi

In the other large shed the noise was almost unbearably loud. Here the fluffy white cotton was having the impurities removed. Lines of women sat feeding the raw cotton into shaking, rattling, screaming machines. This work was terrible; utterly boring and repetitive and carried on in an atmosphere of solid, hellish noise. All conversation was impossible. This, I was told, was the night shift which I think was eight hours long. Five minutes of watching was almost more than I could take.

Mr Bokade and I walked back through the village. The moon was bright and the quiet was a relief. As we walked he asked me about England. He was interested in our divorce rate and talked about arranged marriages and expressed the view that it was a very bad thing that English people treated marriage so lightly.

Back at his house I sat down on the porch again while Mr Bokade supervised the weighing of some cotton that had been brought to his house by a woman. She watched while her load was put on the scales and with her small daughter she collected up fallen bits and pieces and made sure they were included. The scales hung from the ceiling and the weights were heavy stones. When all was completed the woman undid a little knotted cloth at her waist and took from it a handful of pea-pods and put them on the ground before leaving. I guessed the peas were some sort of tally and I asked Mr Bokade why she had left them. He picked one up, shelled it and poured the peas into my hands.

'They are peas,' he said, 'lentils.'

'Why did she leave them?'

'Oh, it's just a little present,' he said, chuckling. 'We let her keep some because we need her work, but she gives us some back as a little present.'

'Does she pick the peas while she is collecting the cotton?'

'Yes, that's right, but we don't mind.'

Mr Bokade was worrying about how I was going to eat my dinner. 'Can you eat with your fingers, like we do?' I had to admit I had not acquired that skill and he arranged for someone to find me a spoon and fork.

'I don't mind trying,' I said, rather looking forward to it. But he waved his hand as if to say, 'Good heavens no.'

Some sleek cows walked across the porch on their way to their quarters. Outside the house a girl squatted by a little decorated stone flower-pot with a plant in it. On the ground she began to draw an intricate pattern of diamonds and star shapes in white lines which she coloured in with bright red, green, blue and black powder that she trickled from her fingers. She worked quickly with confidence and skill. Mrs Nandanwar tried to explain to me, although I couldn't altogether understand, that this was part of a celebration to do with Krishna. She called it an imaginary marriage.

Preparing for Krishna celebration

'You see first Krishna was married, but not really. Then he married his real wife. This, tonight, is the start of the first marriage. The couple can talk to each other, like engaged couples. But it's only imaginary. Later tonight some men will come and sing. You'll see,' she said. I watched the pretty girl and looked at Manisha sitting nearby making a pattern of her own. The grown-ups laughed. 'Look at Manisha; what she is doing is nonsense. It's all wrong.' The elder girl handed Manisha colours when she asked for them but took no notice of the scribble the child was making. She didn't push her away or tell her not to bother her or say, 'Aow! Get her out of it!' as an English older sister might have done to a sibling showing off beside her.

Manisha and her sister

When it was time to eat Mrs Nandanwar announced that I was to go upstairs to eat alone with Mr Bokade because there was a small table and two chairs there. The women and children were to eat downstairs sitting on low stools on the floor, something I could not be expected to do. I looked into the room where the family's meal was laid out and was a bit disappointed not to be joining them. But it looked very difficult to eat like that and any disappointment I felt was also touched with relief that I was not going to have to make a disgusting exhibition of myself. Upstairs a table had been laid in a simple room and delicious food was ready. There was mutton curry, and vegetables and rice and dal and parathas. A spoon and fork were laid for me. Mrs Nandanwar hovered. 'I hope you like Indian food,' she said. 'I love Indian food,' I replied, and explained that for my family it is always a treat to have Indian food in London. She was anxious because she had forgotten to get any drink.

'Perhaps you like whisky or beer?' she said. 'No,' I assured her, 'I do not like to drink with Indian food, I promise you.' She still looked worried.

She put some food on my plate and once we were settled she went downstairs to eat her own dinner.

It was very, very good indeed. The curry was quite hot and made my nose and eyes water but I ate an enormous amount. I couldn't resist it. Mrs Nandanwar came back and I complimented her on the meal.

'It is so good—the best I've had in India.'

She smiled. 'Have some more,' she said, piling up my plate. 'You could use your fork,' she said in a motherly way as I picked up my spoon. She stayed talking with us and brought us up some sweet dessert, a little rice cake in syrup and guavas.

Suddenly she said, 'Come downstairs, you'll see—they are singing.'

Outside by the girl's pattern stood a little group. On the ground were some lamps that were fed now and then with oil. Two children held a piece of cloth stretched between them, like a little curtain hiding the stone flower-pot. The girl and several other men and women, including my driver, stood in a half circle. One man was singing loudly and clearly. Mrs Nandanwar, Mr Bokade and I sat and watched. The atmosphere was playful and merry. The nearest thing to it, I suppose, would be carol singing, except that this scene was set on a warm Indian night and was pagan. Manisha fooled about and didn't apparently do things quite properly, but no one minded. Sometimes the group responded to the singing and clapped or chanted together. Suddenly the cloth was snatched aside and the singing ended. A boy took a lamp and held it out to one of the group. The man held his hands near the flame for a moment and then quickly brushed his hands across his face. The boy held out the lamp to the next person who did the same. He included me in this ritual, quite naturally and without any special smile as if to say, 'Go on, you join in too.' Then he gave each of us a little bit of cake and some flakes of something, chopped nuts perhaps, which were eaten; and that was the end of the pretty ritual.

While we were drinking tea the sound of a car engine being revved came floating through the night.

'Is that my driver?'

'Yes.'

'Does that mean he wants to go?'

'I think it's a sign!'

Mrs Nandanwar gave me a letter for Kranti, and thanked me for coming and for bringing the sweets. She said my visit had made her happy.

'I'm very happy that I came too. Thank you very much for inviting me to dinner. It will be one of my happiest memories of India and I will never forget it.'

Everyone shook hands with me and a boy asked for my autograph. They walked to the car and stood waving in the moonlight as I was driven away. I felt very cheerful and lucky to have spent such a perfect occasion with them all.

All the way along the bumpy track that leads a mile or two to the main road came scores of bullock carts loaded with cotton. The eyes of the animals shone red in the headlights and the drivers swayed as the carts jolted forward. On the main road were still more, coming to feed the gin.

After a while the road became much emptier. Now and then we passed a lorry or a cyclist. People were gathered round fires on the roadside and the dead dog was still there.

The driver went like hell, foot hard down all the way.

From my hotel window, Nagpur, 6.30 a.m.

Calcutta

Monday 29th November

People sweep a lot in India. I looked out of my hotel bathroom window this morning and saw among many other things a woman sweeping the bare earth outside her house. Her broom was a handful of twigs and she raised clouds of dry dust. I watched till she had finished and considered that the yard did look better; neater somehow. On the railway platform this morning I counted at one glance three people sweeping; one was sweeping out a Gents' lavatory, one a bit of platform and the third was sweeping the railway lines. I noticed a little local peculiarity in Nagpur; I observed it later in Calcutta too but cannot remember whether it happened in Delhi as well. It's a very sweet gesture that some Indians make with their heads. It is in exactly equal parts a nod and a shake of the head, which produces (if you try it you'll see) a curious kind of wobble. The gesture has several shades of meaning such as, 'I have heard your order and will now execute it,' or 'I acknowledge your thanks,' or 'That's how it is and I cannot do anything about it.' It manages to be both very final and very polite. I've tried to do it and I can't. You need a looser neck than we Europeans seem to have. Another little habit Indians have (though I'm told it is unknown in the South) is that of punctuating their conversation with the word, or words, '*ahcha*'. Again it has several meanings and is always said softly. It can mean 'Oh dear,' or 'Yes, O.K.,' or 'Well, well,' or 'Oh really.' It is an encouraging little expression, conveying a mild and pleasant goodwill.

There's something very interesting about Indians' English. We tend to think it is merely quaint, but it would be better to think of it as a foreign language. We don't think that Americans *can't* talk proper English just because they use odd expressions, and when Indians mangle our language, it may be a mistake to think they are not making perfectly ordinary sense to each other. A leader in an Indian newspaper said about some recently dead statesman that he had 'emblazoned the horizons of his country.' I suppose in English it should read he emblazoned something on the horizons or he emblazoned the horizons with something but you know perfectly well what the author is getting at without this adjustment. In fact it gives you a fresh look at phrases we take for granted. This Indian version of English has become a language in its own right: it needs a name of its own. It is rich in metaphors and often makes startlingly novel use of phrases and sayings. It is also somewhat convoluted, lending itself to windbaggery.

Nagpur Station

I caught the 10.40 Bombay to Calcutta train and started on the last leg of my Indian journey. The train journey lasted almost twenty-four hours and was very easy and enjoyable. During the daylight I sat by the window as usual and stared at the countryside, which never failed to entertain and interest me.

India seems to be flat from Delhi to Nagpur and from Nagpur to Calcutta, but that does not mean it is monotonous. For one thing I could watch farming. The train does not go terribly fast and I saw peasants cutting grain with sickles, threshing with bullocks drawing a roller round and round in circles, and winnowing by throwing grain into the air from wide wooden bowls for the breeze to catch and carry away the husks. There were women washing clothes in rivers and brilliantly-coloured saris spread out to dry on the banks. I saw a kingfisher, a flash of blue so intense it seemed that all the colour from the immense sky had been crushed into one tiny bird.

On the way to Calcutta

My fellow travellers were just as entertaining as the landscape. A young couple with two toddlers sat near me for most of the journey. They looked after their children very well and the little ones barely cried once although their father described them as very mischievous. The woman was beautiful and fat. She lay down to sleep sometimes, and the children lolled comfortably against her; and when she sat cross-legged her lap made the most wonderful cradle for the smallest child. She played a game with the children, kissing them on their wide open mouths with her own parted lips and then leaning back and smiling lazily.

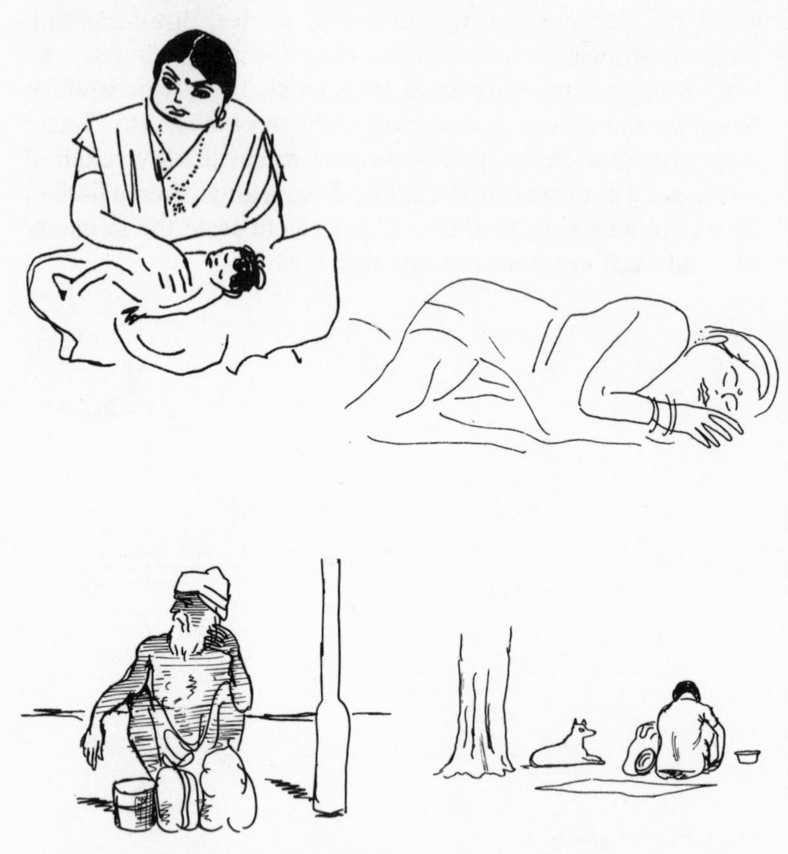

The passengers noticed me drawing whenever the train stopped at stations or elsewhere, and they asked to see and passed my book amongst each other. They spoke to each other in their own language, returning the book to me without comment. They were invariably friendly and helpful, translating when I was ordering food and offering to share with me the food they bought at railway stations.

When night fell I read, lying comfortably in my berth, and I slept well.

One cannot help making comparisons, however misleading and silly they may be, and it seems to me that life in India today must in many places be very like life in 18th and 19th-century England. The crafts that still thrive, the traditional ways of life that are still intact, and the great variety of occupation and costume and dialect remind one of accounts of English life of the last two centuries. All that richness has long vanished from England, except where it has been revived by some local group or organisation nostalgically clinging to the past. Seeing it here is unforgettable. I would not of course enjoy the hardships of being poor in India, but there's no denying the pleasure to be got from seeing the past in this way. Dickens comes to life before your eyes in the cities; in the country perhaps John Clare is more accurate. It has occurred to me that once India makes it just slightly easier to get about, jet planes will bring half Europe here on holiday trips and the whole thing will in turn become swamped and utterly changed. (A few moments after I had jotted this notion down, the idea that a few European holiday-makers could ever change this vast sub-continent seemed absolutely ludicrous.)

When I woke up in the morning at about six and looked out of the window the landscape had changed. In the misty light I could see many more palm trees and what I think were paddy fields. The country was criss-crossed by little irrigation canals and there were many ponds or little lakes. The small fields looked neat and well-tended. The whole aspect was tranquil and pretty.

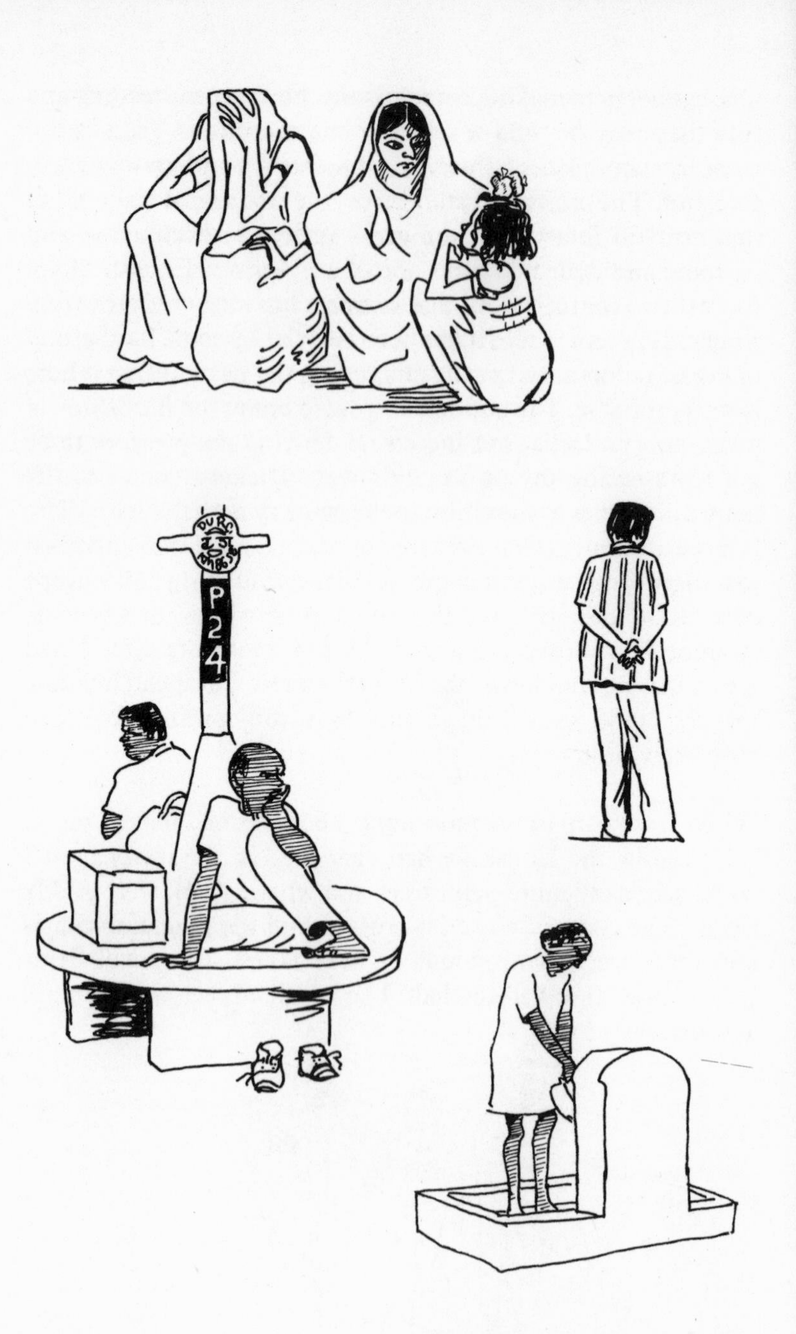

From the train on the way to Calcutta

Tea was ordered and the family in my compartment kindly paid for mine. A sweeper came down the corridor cleaning the already perfectly clean floor. I saw a goat with a jackdaw on its back standing in a garden. We began to pass through small stations crowded with passengers waiting for commuter trains to take them into Calcutta. We passed a few of these trains. They chuffed rather sedately along with the doors of the carriages open. Some passengers sat with their legs dangling outside while others were crammed inside. It was like a hint about what to expect in Calcutta. Several friends had said to me, 'You must go to Calcutta, but don't go there first. Acclimatise yourself to India for as long as you can before you visit Calcutta, otherwise the shock may be too great.'

Actually the station was no more and no less crowded than any other station in India—that is to say it was absolutely jam-packed.

Outside Calcutta

Tuesday 30th November

As usual a porter appeared and grabbed my bag before I stepped down from the train. He swung one bag up onto his head and indicated to me that I should lift my other bag onto the top of that one. I followed him through the crowd and was instantly picked up by a driver. This was an error. It turned out to be not a meter taxi but a sort of freelance cab and therefore driven by an even greater crook than usual. In no time my bags were locked in the boot, but I didn't get in the car.

'Oberoi Grand,' I said. 'How much?'

'One hundred rupees,' said the driver matter-of-factly. I was furious. I got hold of the handle of the boot and wrenched it to and fro as hard as I could, hoping the crummy thing would snap off and I'd bust the lock.

'Fifty rupees,' said the driver.

'Open the fucking boot before I kick it in,' I said.

'Forty,' he said, getting into the driver's seat. I stayed where I was. He got out again.

'O.K., I find a full car,' he said, and disappeared into the crowd to find more passengers. I tried to open the boot, watched by some interested passers-by. In a moment the driver was back.

'O.K. Thirty rupees,' he said.

'Open this boot,' I said grimly. I found I was enjoying this absurd scene. A few yards away proper taxis were accepting passengers, turning on their meters and driving off.

'No, no, come on, thirty rupees.'

'O.K., twenty,' I said.

'Thirty—I have no full car.'

'Twenty.'

'I have no full car.'

'Twenty.'

'O.K.'

We crossed the Hooghly river and I realised I was on the famous Howrah Bridge. There is a special sensation caused by finding that you are somewhere already familiar from pictures and literature. It is a delightfully mixed feeling. In one way the actual reality of the place strikes you with vivid clarity; in another way you feel a dreamlike sense of having somehow entered a fairy-tale world and become part of the stories or pictures that previously described the scene to you.

The driver used the mad technique of swerving and honking that all drivers use in India and soon arrived at the hotel. The street is not particularly grand and one side of it is all dug up at the moment because part of a new underground railway is being constructed there.

I paid my driver, who seemed perfectly content. He'd probably rooked me anyway. A doorman, splendidly got up with a red turban, red sash and white uniform, motioned to me to put down my bags until he'd summoned a porter, but I could not be bothered to wait and carried my luggage into the hotel. Instantly the roaring, dusty, hot street vanished. One step past the doorman and the world became cool, ordered and silent. For all that I'd said, and felt, in Nagpur about luxury hotels being unreal and a bit boring, how welcome it was to be shown to a comfortable room, to have a hot bath, to put on clean clothes and to go down to a pretty restaurant by a swimming pool shaded by graceful palm trees, and to have coffee and croissants.

After breakfast I telephoned M. J. Akbar. Arun Shourie had given me his number and said Akbar could fix anything and that I should call him as soon as I arrived.

He is a young editor, who had very successfully started two journals, the weekly *Sunday* and the daily *Telegraph*. Arun described him as a bit of a tearaway, ambitious and tough. 'Anything you want, anyone you want to meet, just ask Akbar.'

When I rang the *Telegraph* office I was told that the editor would not be in until 4.30, so I rang Akbar's home number. He sounded extremely sleepy on the phone, but said he'd meet me at midday at his office. He said I could walk to the office and told me how to find it. I discovered later that he works until two to three each morning and that I had woken him from his desperately-needed morning sleep.

I set out in plenty of time in order to do some drawing and look around. The atmosphere in Calcutta was different from Delhi but I could not define how. Perhaps it was the absence of the Lutyens government buildings and the special air of a capital city; perhaps it was that Delhi had been cleaned up for the Asian Games and Calcutta was its usual battered self. Perhaps I was different. I felt very relaxed and confident. I had arrived at my jumping-off place; this was my last stop and I felt pleased with myself for having done it all and got this far without any disasters.

Calcutta

The streets were not only more crowded than Delhi, New Delhi that is, but also much narrower. The buildings rose higgledy-piggledy from the dust. Wobbly verandas leant out from the upper storeys, incredibly dirty windows were half obscured by corrugated-iron additions or enormous cinema hoardings, power and telephone wires looped and dangled from leaning posts and rusty hooks. It all looked decayed and old, yet solid in some contradictory way, as if there was a hell of a lot more decay where that came from. There's a lot more crumbling in the old place yet.

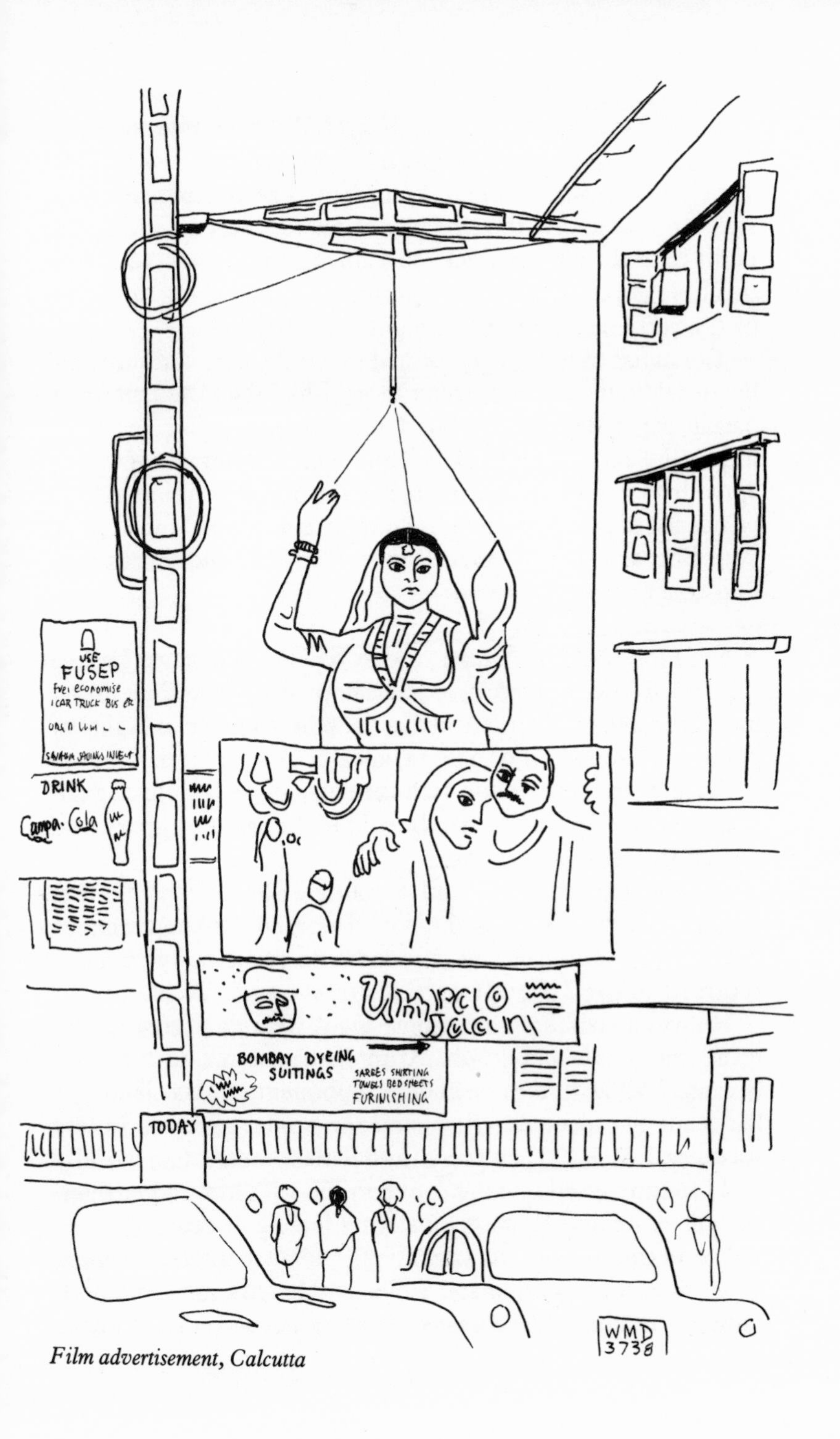

Film advertisement, Calcutta

There were not the teeming beggars I'd been told to expect but there were plenty of people living on the pavements. Some slept, some cooked or minded children. There were many food stalls and shops and the air smelt of coal or charcoal smoke. At night-time the air was thick with smoke and I was told that at this time of year smog is a big problem, often making travelling in the early morning and at night very difficult.

The mood of the streets seemed to me cheerful and busy and hectic. Perhaps it is too strong to say I had the impression of a barely controlled mania, but I felt something like that; not unlike the excitement in New York. You feel something pretty appalling may be going to happen in the near future and instead of a sense of dismay something nearer to a carnival mood grips you. But, as I said, I was feeling high anyway and this may be nonsense.

When I got to the *Telegraph*, Akbar had not arrived so I asked the way to the nearest, best bookshop. For some time now I have been extremely interested in the school known as Kalighat painting. I hoped I'd be able to buy a book about it in Calcutta because it was here, in the 19th century, at the temple of Kali, that the painting was done to be sold to the many pilgrims who visited the temple every year.

I found the bookshop and a young assistant told me that although he did not stock the book I wanted, he knew where I could find it and gave me directions to two nearby shops. I returned to the *Telegraph* and this time found Akbar.

He was a strikingly handsome man, wearing a grey jersey, jeans and sandals. Because Arun had sent me to him and because I knew him to be another opponent of Mrs Gandhi, I had vaguely expected to find someone similar to Arun. But he was very different. He was civil and patient rather than friendly and I found myself making conversation with him rather than, as with Arun and Romesh, instantly feeling at ease.

We began at once to talk about Indian politics, meaning government, corruption and violence. He gave me some back numbers of his weekly *Sunday*, pointing out accounts of police brutality and government crime. It all tallied exactly with Arun's stories and it was horrifying. There were numerous examples of official terrorism, beatings, threats and brutal murders, as well as bribery and fraud. Again I puzzled over the fact that all this, such common knowledge in India, is so little reported in Europe.

After a while, almost for want of something to say, I asked him whether he could help me with a task my father-in-law had given me. In 1981 Calcutta University had awarded my father-in-law a gold medal. For various reasons he had not been able to come to Calcutta to receive it and had, therefore, asked for it to be posted to him. As it had never arrived he had wondered if I might try to get it for him.

Akbar listened to this story and quickly made two phone calls. He made some notes on a piece of paper.

'Go now,' he said, 'to this address and ask for Professor Chatterjee. He will help you.' It was so abrupt I felt almost as if I was being dismissed. 'You must be there in twenty minutes or so; you'll make it. Come back here this evening. We'll do something, fix something up.'

I thanked him and left to look for a taxi. Akbar had behaved with the utmost correctness, had been very helpful, and had invited me back. Nevertheless I went away with a faint feeling that it had all been a bit of a bore for him and I found his cool manner slightly alarming.

The taxi dropped me outside the University and I paused on the pavement to check Akbar's directions. Two students, a boy and a girl, hurried up to me. The boy held out a little square of black material and a pin. They wanted me to wear it as a sign of mourning for their beloved leader who had died that day, and whom I understood was a Communist.

'I'm sorry,' I blurted out, 'I don't wear black for Communists.' They both looked embarrassed. The boy continued for a moment to hold out the black square, then turned and walked away. The girl stayed, looking at me.

'Can you tell me how to find this building?' I asked her,

showing her Akbar's note; and she pointed it out to me, smiling.

I ascended a dark staircase and arrived at a more or less deserted floor. Doors gave off the corridor to dim and dusty rooms but there was little sign of life and I began to think I'd come to the wrong place. I stopped the first man I saw.

'Excuse me, I'm looking for Professor Chatterjee.'

He frowned and shook his head and went on. I asked a couple more people and at last found one with a glimmer of some understanding who said, 'Follow me.'

He led me to an ancient notice-board on which was pinned a yellowing, curled-up, faded piece of paper. He blew and wiped away a layer of dust and peered for some time at the words that were still just readable.

'Professor Chatterjee will not be here until four thirty,' he said finally.

'I think that must be the wrong Professor Chatterjee,' I said.

'There is only one,' he remarked.

'Thank you,' I said. For another five minutes or so I roamed the floor, stopping everyone I met and asking always for the elusive Professor. Some said there was no such person, some said he existed but they knew not where, some racked their brains and asked others on my behalf and some shrugged. None of this made me doubt that I'd find him. I was certain of Akbar's reliability.

I paused at the head of a staircase and from the shadows a man approached. 'Mr Garland? I've been looking for you—Professor Chatterjee,' he said. It turned out I'd been on the right floor, but on the wrong side of the large building. News of my search had spread.

The Professor took me to the office of Mr Jagadiswar Pal, the Estates and Trust Officer of Calcutta University. He sat in a tall dark office full of filing cabinets and heaps of old papers and folders. The room looked as if it had not been touched since 1857 when it was built. It was quiet and cool and comfortable. Mr Pal ordered some tea and listened to my story. I showed him a letter from my father-in-law spelling out the means by which I should try to recover the medal. The letter was slightly jokey and I hoped the serious Mr Pal was not going to be offended by it.

When he had read it he said that he'd been trying to get the medal to England for a year but all sorts of bureaucratic problems had so far prevented its dispatch. Now only one small problem remained: he needed a letter of authority, preferably from my father-in-law, giving him permission to hand the medal over to me.

'Well,' I said, 'I can identify myself. I have my passport with me, for instance, and you have in your hand a letter from my father-in-law.'

'Ah,' he said, 'but this is a private letter to you and will not do for my files.'

I remembered that I had the name of Robin Twite, the head of the British Council here, and I felt sure he would solve the problem for me. I suggested to Mr Pal that perhaps Mr Twite would help.

Mr Pal smiled and said eagerly, 'Oh, you know Mr Twite,' as if that meant our troubles were over. We telephoned him and it was arranged I should go there this afternoon, pick up a letter of authority from him, return with it on Thursday afternoon at 3.00, and the medal would be handed over.

Mr Pal and I shook hands and I went out into the bright sunshine.

This whole incident seemed to me typical of India. There had been a certain vagueness about it. Did Professor Chatterjee exist or not? Was the medal here at all? Could Mr Pal hand it over to me without more authority? Yet these uncertainties, if approached calmly and unhurriedly, disappear. So long as you adapt your tempo to the country and people not only are things possible, but they are accomplished in a pleasantly old-fashioned way that includes tea and talk and idle waiting that is not without its pleasures. But you do need to be patient, and usually to accept the need to go elsewhere for some bureaucratic reason, before returning and finally completing your business.

Once outside I remembered another task a friend had set me. It was to discover any reference that may exist to a certain Mr Esdaile, who in 1833 set up a Mesmeric hospital in Mott Street in Calcutta. It occurred to me that the University where I now was might be the best place to start looking. As I paused a man who was passing noticed me and said politely, 'May I help you?' He was in his early thirties and spoke very good English.

'Well, I'm not sure,' I said and explained my unusual problem. He listened to me and said, 'Have you time to come to my office? Would you like a cup of tea?'

His name is Mr Chakravorti and he works in the Institute of Hygiene and Public Health, in the Industrial Hygiene Department. He is a psychologist. As my wife is a psychologist and my father used to work in Industrial Health, conversation was exceptionally easy. Among other things, I told him of my search for a book on Kalighat paintings and asked him how far it was to the Kalighat Temple itself.

'Do you want to go there?' he asked.

'Oh yes, very much,' I replied.

'Would you like me to accompany you there?'

'That's awfully kind of you—when?'

'Now,' he said, as if surprised I should ask.

'But aren't you working?'

'Oh, I can fix that; I must just telephone a colleague.' He made a couple of phone calls and soon we were in a taxi.

Again this is typical of India. People seem to be prepared to find time for unexpected visits or conversations and be much more ready to change their plans than we are. Obviously this meant that sometimes meetings are missed, officials are absent and difficulties are caused, but it also means that all kinds of opportunities are taken that in England would be missed. Hospitality means more in India: it includes the suggestion 'I will put myself out for you,' as well as, 'I will be welcoming,' which is what we usually mean and which is not the same thing at all.

Kalighat was one of the few places in India that I had read about and knew a bit about, and therefore had an idea of what to expect. Needless to say, it took me completely by surprise. I had expected a large reddish-grey building standing alone. I found a smallish pale building with brilliantly coloured details that was half-hidden by surrounding walls and outbuildings. I had expected the old stalls and memento-sellers (where once the Kalighat paintings had been on sale) to have vanished by so late in the 20th century; but they were all there, and thriving, and selling the same sort of thing, except that now the lovely water-colour paintings were replaced by ugly reproductions of fifth-rate pictures. There were a few beggars and a number of tourists but no other Europeans.

Mr Chakravorti guided me through the little alleys to the entrance of the temple where we left our shoes and went in. 'On certain days,' he said, 'great crowds come here to worship Kali. They sacrifice goats and get very worked up. The whole place,' he gestured round the courtyard, 'runs in blood.' He smiled almost apologetically.

'Have you seen it?' I asked.

He pulled a face and shook his head. 'I don't like that sort of thing,' he said.

Kalighat Temple, Calcutta

'Do people get hurt?' I asked, conjuring up a picture of bloody frenzy and the terrifying black figure of Kali driving the faithful to acts of violence against one another.

'Oh yes, in the crowd; they get crushed you know.' At least they don't slit each others' throats.

Away from the temple we walked to where some steps led down to a narrow river. Mr Chakravorti explained that this was the old course of the Ganges, but that the river had changed its course and now only this small part of it still flowed here. A ferry plied to and fro across the dirty, yellow-green water and from the steps men, women and children bathed and splashed, some completely immersing themselves and coming up dripping and squirting out mouthfuls of Ganges. God only knows what a teaspoon of that stuff would do to a European.

I watched a pretty girl filling several jars and plastic containers with the dirty water. A few yards away in midstream a dead thing floated by. It was impossible to see what it had been; human, dog or sheep. On its back and clear of the water rode a jackdaw, tearing busily at the sodden, rotting flesh.

Collecting Ganges water, Kalighat, Calcutta

'That girl is collecting water for home purification and domestic worship,' said Mr Chakravorti. 'This is a very holy place for them.' He indicated the people. 'For them this water will purify, and yet,' he gestured to the right, 'they will also defecate into it.' Long wreaths of orange marigolds swirled past, and the pretty girl stepped deeper into the water, and sprinkled droplets over her head with a graceful sweeping movement of her hand.

Near the steps were several statues, each of the same two figures: a woman with her hands together as if in prayer, cradling in her lap the head of a man who lay dead. This couple were Savitri and Satyavan. Savitri is worshipped as the ideal married lady who by her virtue and purity was able to bring her husband Satyavan back to life after he died of a snake-bite. She bathed his body in the Ganges and prayed until the gods gave life back to him. Each representation of these figures was covered with brilliant vermilion powder and scattered coins. As I watched, a woman leant down, picked up some of the powder and rubbed it on Savitri.

'See, she is worshipping,' murmured Mr Chakravorti.

'Who takes the money?' I asked.

'Those who look after the shrine.'

Savitri and Satyavan

I bought some bracelets made of conch shell and one or two other odds and ends. Mr Chakravorti bargained for me. As we moved away he and the stallkeeper seemed to share a little joke.

'He is saying that normally he'd expect thirty rupees for that lot,' smiled Mr Chakravorti, nodding his head at my fifteen-rupee purchases.

I handed the few coins I'd received in change into the passively outstretched hands of some little children. They at once became extremely animated, crying out and tugging at my clothes and waving their arms frantically while their faces contorted into pleading grimaces.

Mr Chakravorti too became agitated.

'Don't give them any more,' he hissed. 'Your life will be unbearable.' He strode away fast, scattering the children and speaking to them sharply in their own language.

Our taxi had waited for us and we drove to Mr Twite's address. On the way, my new friend said, 'If there is anything I can do for you while you are in Calcutta, please let me know, and next time you come, if you'd like to see how we middle-class live, perhaps you'll come to dinner with us.'

I spent the next couple of hours in a very different sort of India. Mr Twite, the head of the British Council in Calcutta, lives in a huge flat in an enormous house built sometime in the last eight years by an Indian maharajah or millionaire. In this household, surrounded by servants and Indian *objets d'art*, a bit of the old British India is kept intact. I do not mean that Mr Twite has immense political powers or that he rules anywhere, but the atmosphere of isolated European privilege is strong and it is flavoured by a mixture of affection for certain aspects of Indian life, particularly Indian art, and a degree of contempt for Indian muddle and inefficiency. All this is expressed with a lofty, smiling but, I felt, somewhat patronising goodwill.

This quality is difficult to describe without sounding more critical than I feel. It may be necessary if you are going to live and work in India to be a lot less starry-eyed about it than I am and can afford to be. When I put to Mr Twite some of Arun

Shourie's tales of the violence of Indian political life, he more or less said that he thought Mr Shourie was exaggerating. 'You see, India is so big; there are areas so remote; this sort of thing is bound to happen . . .'

Somehow Arun and corrupt politicians and police murder squads were all part of India, and jolly baffling too. This attitude, if I diagnosed it correctly, jarred on me; but at the same time I knew Mr Twite could not do anything about it and it certainly wasn't his fault, and it would have been idiotic for the two of us to have sat there raging about the horror of it all.

Mr Twite noticed my interest in a primitive painting that hung in his office. It was in the form of a long scroll made up of separate framed scenes. He explained that it was a storyteller's prop—that each scene illustrated a moment in a tale and was shown at the appropriate moment as the story was told. 'I've got another,' he said. 'You can have it if you like.' He went out and returned with a similar scroll. I could hardly believe it and thanked him very much.

'Oh, it's not very good I'm afraid,' he said, waving away my thanks. 'Someone brought it to me and I gave him a few rupees for it—I think the old skills have largely been lost you know . . .'

He made a note of what to write to Mr Pal in order for me to get the gold medal, and took me to meet his wife.

We sat in a lovely sitting room and drank lime soda and talked; about Michael Holroyd's biography of Augustus John and about London and newspapers and very British matters, as the afternoon light faded outside.

I said I was going to have to get back to my hotel and grab something to eat before going to meet Akbar.

'Oh, we'll rustle something up,' said Mr Twite.

A servant appeared a few moments later with some cheese on toast. I felt extraordinarily content. Everything was so utterly familiar and secure and relaxed.

'I'll get the car to run you back to your hotel when you are ready to go,' said Mr Twite. They invited me to lunch on Thursday and said I could pick up my letter for Mr Pal before taking it straight up to him after lunch.

The smooth, comfortable and clean official car was quite different to the bouncing, honking taxis I'd become used to. I sat back and looked out of the window at the chaotic scenes outside. I felt sealed-off. I felt a new expression on my face, more haughty, less wary; Walter Mitty-like, I was able for the moment to be a British ruler, swept through the dirty streets in luxurious security.

From the hotel, where I dumped my drawing things, I walked to Akbar's office. The streets were just as crowded and busy by night as they had been by day, slightly busier if anything. Off the main road people slept on the pavement. I saw two small children curled up, apparently alone and fast asleep. Near them was piled some cooking equipment which suggested there were some parents somewhere who would return sometime. I remember years ago puzzling about how affluent Victorians could have lived contentedly alongside the starving poor of 19th-century England. I saw in a flash how easy it must have been. Short of a vague thought that I hoped the sleeping infants were all right, I simply did not consider their plight for a moment, and even if they had definitely not been all right, whatever that might have meant, I could not have done anything.

The night air was thick with coal smoke. It made me cough and reminded me of London in the fifties. Akbar, still cool and slightly remote, took me by car to his flat some distance away, in the south of the city I think. We drove along talking about this and that. When we arrived at the block where he lived, he apologised for the lift's slowness. It is worked off a generator (because otherwise the power cuts would too often render it useless), but the generator is not strong enough to get it to work very well.

Inside the large sprawling flat I could hear other people and glimpsed a woman and a child whom I took to be servants as I was shown into Akbar's study. On the floor was a mattress and bedding. Akbar explained that he slept here sometimes when he got home particularly late. The woman I'd seen came in with the child, a little girl of twelve or so. They tried to pick up the mattress to take it out of our way. I had to restrain myself from helping, as giggling and whispering they failed to manage the awkward task. Akbar also watched for a few moments, then picked it up himself and carried it out. The woman and child trotted out after him, tittering with embarrassment.

When Akbar came back his small daughter came and sat on his lap, while he hugged her and stroked her hair. He said that he tries to take a break from his office about this time of night and if he can, comes home to spend some time with his two children. Later his chubby baby also got a cuddle.

After a bit his wife, Mallika, joined us and conversation began to get easier. They drank rum and I drank whisky. A grey poodle wandered around the room.

'Look at it,' said Mallika. 'It's supposed to be a *white* poodle,' she laughed. Tiring of talking politics, I asked Mallika what her job was.

'She was a journalist when we met,' said Akbar.

'Now I am training to become a psychoanalyst,' said Mallika.

'Really,' I said. 'So is my wife.'

This discovery broke the ice in an amazing way. An extremely animated and humorous, but very interesting conversation began about the various difficulties that psychoanalytic training can produce, in family and social life. It is a theme I have often heard discussed in my own house and it was obviously familiar to them. The fact that we shared this experience brought us together and seemed to relax Akbar considerably, even more than the rum perhaps.

He said, 'I want to tell you something frankly. When I heard I was going to have to entertain an English journalist from the *Daily Telegraph* I thought "Oh no!" I was dreading it. But this is a marvellous evening. I'm really enjoying it!' He looked quite different. All trace of exhaustion had gone; he laughed and waved his arms and sometimes became very serious. 'Come, have another drink,' he said. 'We often have to take a lot of shit from English journalists, telling us what is wrong with India!'

We talked about Arun and Romesh. He was critical of

Romesh. 'He is from the same generation and class as Mrs Gandhi. He's no different from them really, it's just that he never became a minister, so he now attacks her. Raj is very bright,' he added.

I couldn't understand this: Romesh had seemed to me an articulate and implacable enemy of Mrs Gandhi; but Akbar went on to talk about Arun.

First he described their similarities. 'We are both products of the emergency, which threw up a new, outspoken form of journalism. We are established now and cannot be silenced.'

'Arun has been silenced,' I said.

'That's different. He's not really a journalist in one way. He'll go on into politics now. And he'll be successful. He will be influential in the future development of India.' He paused. 'There will come a time when I will have to oppose him.'

'What do you mean?' I asked. Akbar began a long, rambling and obscure speech that I entirely failed to make sense of. It touched on the fact that Arun is a Hindu and Akbar a Moslem. Mallika watched him, smiling, and told him, 'You are being very vague.'

'Is he afraid of sounding disloyal to Arun?' I asked Mallika. She smiled. 'Not quite.'

Akbar frowned and looked uncomfortable.

'If there is something you don't want to say, don't say it,' I told him.

'Arun does not care enough about people, you know,' said Akbar, after a moment. 'He cares about issues and politics. He is like a chess player. He is too cold, too calculating. He's only interested in getting rid of Indira Gandhi.' Admiration, respect and affection for Arun battled in Akbar with some conflict that he was unable or perhaps loathe to explain to me.

Mallika said, 'There are tremendously deep feelings against Moslems in India. I am a Christian and was brought up in a liberal family. There was never any question that I would have to marry anyone but a man of my own choice. But when I said I was going to marry Akbar, my mother said, "But darling, they can have *four* wives, and they treat them all so badly."'

She smiled.

I gave up. This additional complication of religious differences was more than I could attempt to understand at this time of night and after three whiskies.

Fragments of this evening's conversations come back to me.

AKBAR: The idea of Indians being non-violent is ludicrous; they are extremely violent. Inter-caste violence shows it—horribly.

AKBAR: Do you know the one thing I admire about the British? Their balls!

ME: And Shakespeare.

AKBAR: Yes and Shakespeare.

ME: And cricket.

AKBAR: Ah, cricket. (*He begins to laugh.*)

ME: And their sense of fair play!

AKBAR (*laughing out loud*): And their sense of fair play!

AKBAR: India is no longer interested in England for any practical purposes. France, yes, and the U.S.S.R.

ME: Not even after the Falklands War?

MALLIKA: Especially not after the Falklands War. We disapproved of that very much, you know.

AKBAR: The Festival of India was a failure and had nothing to do with promoting anything but Mrs Gandhi's attempt to become an important world figure. She wants to be an international leader like Tito or Nasser!

MALLIKA (*When I said I wished they could come to my house in London*): We cannot afford to travel. We are too poor.

AKBAR: We come from lower middle-class backgrounds. It is only recently that we could afford an apartment like this. It is because of my job we've got this now. When we first married, such a place was our dream.

Akbar dropped me off at the hotel at about midnight, on his way back to work. He told me to call round tomorrow evening at about 7.00 at his office—'and we'll fix something up.'

Throughout this evening's conversation, whenever the topic was India or concerned Indian matters, I was aware that I was expressing a very romantic and therefore unrealistic view. Both Akbar and Mallika let me know that they thought so too, but not aggressively. With little smiles and nods and by letting things I said pass without comment they often seemed to be saying, 'You'll learn.'

Wednesday 1st December

For once today I had a clear plan of what I wanted to do and set out from the hotel at about 9.00 in the morning. First I was going to find the bookshop where I could buy the book on Kalighat painting. Next I was going to the Academy of Fine Art, and a museum that is nearby, to see some Kalighat pictures. I was going to visit the Victoria Memorial and then take a taxi ride round Calcutta to orientate myself generally. This itinerary would leave time to take advantage of any unexpected possibilities that might turn up.

But first of all I could not find the bookshop. I followed the directions carefully but each street was like the last, crowded and busy, full of stalls and shops and skinny rickshaw boys, but without the landmarks I'd been told to expect. I didn't really mind to begin with. I did a drawing or two, watched by a curious bunch of passers-by. As I was completing one drawing, a splotch of bird-dropping splashed over the page and onto my clothes. I cursed violently. The boys watching me did not laugh or appear to enjoy my discomfort and rage; one of them thoughtfully gestured to me to move a yard or two away from the arch under which I was standing. I felt very touched by their solemn and sympathetic reaction.

I asked a passer-by to direct me to a bookshop and received

Calcutta

more instructions, and at last found my original target. But it wasn't a bookshop. It was a sort of mail-order office. There were a few books in a dark room upstairs and in a candle-lit space off a landing there was a lending library. A helpful young man said they had nothing on Kalighat painting. He had had such a book in stock but no longer. He told me about two other shops that would definitely have copies. His directions were clear and the next time it was a proper bookshop, but I was told they had nothing on the Kalighat school. I tried the other and received the same reply. Once more two other shops were mentioned to me and I walked off, dimly realising I was on a wild goose chase but also determined not to admit defeat yet.

Out in the street I saw, for the first time, one or two of the famed Calcutta beggars, men whose deformed bodies gave them the appearance of weird animals. Their legs grew from the wrong places or were twisted into bizarre and useless shapes. I saw a boy of perhaps ten lying asleep on a piece of dirty cloth. He had no legs. A blind young man sat stroking a large boulder that seemed to be his only possession. Another blind boy pensively touched his own penis which, although covered by the folds of his ragged clothing, stuck out erect and enormous. It was not clear to me whether he was comforting himself or whether this display was part of his begging act.

The next bookshop I found was closed for stock-taking. I asked there anyway but without any luck. The second shop was so dimly lit inside that there were candles placed near some of the shelves, it also had nothing for me.

Outside on the blazing pavement I felt the frustration and exasperation that old hands at India had warned me about. It was as if the bookshop staff were doing it on purpose, deliberately wasting my time and ruining my day.

After all my walking and searching I was now back at a point only a couple of blocks away from my hotel, and most of the morning had gone. I bought some beautiful notebooks so that I'd feel the day had not been utterly useless. I left them at the hotel, drank a fresh lime and soda and set out again. There was one more bookshop and it was in the direction of the Academy.

I was followed by a shoe-shine boy. 'Sir, sir, your shoes are very dirty. Only one rupee sir. Sir, you are my first customer.'

I stopped to do a drawing. The shoe-shine boy joined the crowd watching. He stood right in front of me and I asked him to move slightly. He shifted to one side and laughed and said, 'Shoe-shine?'

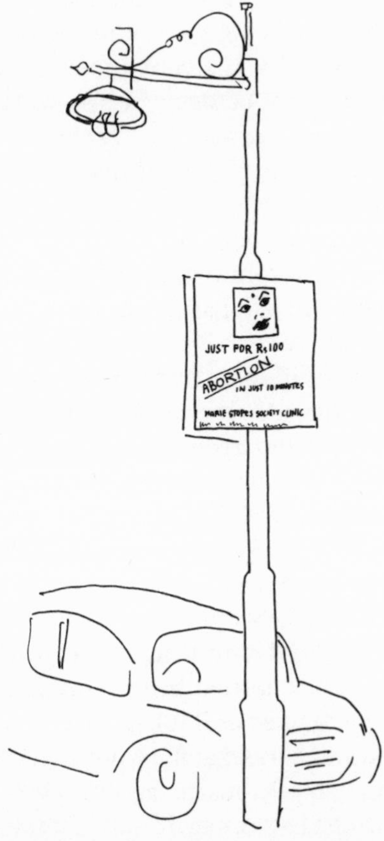

Calcutta

Further down the street a rickshaw man, quite an old man, left his rickshaw and hurried after me. I could not hear what he was saying at first, then I understood: 'Girl? Girl?'

'Did you say girl?'

'Yes, yes, pretty girl, blue dance,' he said urgently, making a curving gesture with one hand.

'No thanks.'

At the bookshop I found two small books on Kalighat painting. One was an unillustrated pamphlet rather than a book, the other a book on Kalighat drawing. An unusually rude and off-hand assistant told me he had nothing else and that the only other existing book was the catalogue of the collection of Kalighat pictures at the V & A in London.

'Many bookshops have told me other books exist,' I said.

'Why didn't they sell you a copy then?' he said coolly.

'Because they were out of stock,' I hissed. He seemed to be positively enjoying my rage and the power it gave him over me. He shrugged dismissively. I gritted my teeth and bought the book of drawings.

I gave up looking for books after that and took a taxi to the Art Gallery. It was closed until 3.00 and it was now only 2.00. I decided to go back to Kalighat for an hour.

I think of all the places in India that I visited this temple was the most exciting and strange. It truly had an air of mystery and menace for me that I found irresistible. It was mainly its association with Kalighat painting; but it was also the presence of the bloody and frightening Kali herself; and it had to do with the beggars and the awful dogs, the dirt and crowded stalls and the yellowy-green Ganges swirling by. It is an ancient holy place where the faithful still worship.

I sat on a step and did a drawing, while little naked beggar children whispered and jostled behind me and a hairless dog with crazy eyes that looked as if it had been designed by Ralph Steadman, glared and barked at me from a safe distance. It was a horrible creature, black, insane and malevolent.

I went to watch the bathers again and bought a yellow plastic toy lion with a gaping red mouth and red eyes and mane.

When I returned to the Academy it was still not open although it was past 3.00. A man in a *dhoti* invited me for tea while I waited.

'I'm in charge here,' he said. 'I'll show you round.' I said I really wanted to see his Kalighat pictures. He became vague.

When we entered the Gallery he walked along behind me,

smoking and intoning the names of the modern artists whose work we were passing. He was unwilling to let me miss one. I was feeling fed up with him and the work which all looked like rubbish. It was mostly an unsatisfactory muddle of undigested European influences and it all looked very much the same.

Some large ancient paintings on silk were pinned up inside enormous shiny plastic envelopes. The plastic had discoloured with age and these exhibits were quite literally invisible.

A large collection of gouache paintings by the distinguished artist Jamini Roy were framed and mounted but unglazed. They were gathering a thick layer of dirt that floated in through open windows and they were curling out of their frames in the heat.

'You ought to put glass over these pictures,' I said.

'Oh this is only a temporary exhibition,' said my guide airily.

It turned out there were no Kalighat-school pictures in the Gallery. There were some lovely old miniatures and Company Period pictures but they were very badly hung, poorly lit and difficult to see.

I walked from the Gallery across the road towards the Victoria Memorial. It squatted on the ground rather than rose from it. Only its size was impressive. There was something almost pathetic about it and about the statues of British heroes of the day that guarded it. It was such a confident statement about the British rule in India which had turned out in the end to be so temporary. The statues, frozen in their arrogance, had egg all over their faces.

It was too late by now for my planned taxi ride round Calcutta. I went back to the hotel feeling the day had all gone wrong and mildly fed up with myself for doing so badly.

When later I walked round to Akbar's office I found to my relief he was out. I left him a half-bottle of scotch that I'd been carrying around all over India and a note saying I'd ring later, and then returned to the Oberoi.

I spent the evening writing. When I rang Akbar he suggested we meet the following night. 'Come at, say, seven thirty. We'll go and meet some friends, perhaps go to Chinatown, see the night life. We'll fix something . . .'

Later I rang Caroline and the boys and felt wildly elated after making contact with them and hearing, for the first time in nearly three weeks, that they were all fine.

Thursday 2nd December

When I looked out of the window this morning the day was misty, but it was one of those days when you know that above the mist is clear sky and hot sun.

I took a taxi down to the river. I wanted to see the Howrah Bridge again, and more of the town. When the taxi reached a certain point I asked him to stop and wait for me, and walked to a busy archway through which I could see steps and beyond them the river. The slippery steps led down to a muddy strand crowded with men and boys bathing and washing in the brownish-yellow water.

The broad river was dotted with boats. Little skiffs pointed at both ends, great flat barges, launches and ferries and black

Babughat, near Howrah Bridge, Calcutta

sailing boats with square red sails. Some men were shovelling mud into wheelbarrows although I could not see why. Shifting it from one place to another seemed pointless. Everything was covered with shiny mud. I had to walk very carefully across the steps so as not to fall. I drew a picture of the scene but decided to move on because I could not see the Howrah Bridge from where I was and although the place was pretty and I wanted to watch the bathers and mud shovellers, there was nowhere to sit.

I told the taxi driver to go on towards the Howrah Bridge and when I saw it looming up before me, I stopped the car and got out. The driver virtually doubled the charge that was on the meter. By now I didn't even argue, I just gave him half; and he didn't argue either, he just took it.

I thought at first I was going to find a dockside or wharf as I threaded my way through some warehouse-like buildings towards the river, but I suddenly emerged onto a flat dusty area that sloped gently down to the river some twenty or thirty yards away. On my left were trees and to my right more buildings and just beyond them the mighty Howrah Bridge, shining dully through the still, hazy morning air. The whole place was swarming with people.

Under the trees a dozen or so great naked giants lay sprawling and chatting on the ground. Later I discovered they were wrestlers. They wore tiny g-strings and were a strange pale colour from the dust that covered them from head to foot. Some of them were doing slow lazy exercises and others were being massaged by smaller men. One lay like an elephant while a man walked up and down on his back or from time to time fell on his knees and drove his hands deep into the huge muscles of the monster's legs and shoulders. Also under the trees were a group of much more active men. They were doing vigorous exercises such as push-ups and knee-bends, and swinging heavy dumb-bells. Their powerful bodies were oiled and shone dark brown. At the water's edge a thick crowd of men bathed and splashed and washed clothes and near to where I stood, scores of people dried clothes, slept, chatted and sat; some beggars, some looking quite prosperous and comfortable.

With a kind of shock I suddenly noticed that the bridge which looked so huge and still was actually alive with people. It was like realising that you are standing right on top of an ant's nest and that what you thought was solid ground is in fact seething animal life. Right across the bridge, not just crowded together, but jammed shoulder to shoulder, moved a solid stream of people. I was too far away to pick out individuals; all I could see was endless movement.

I sat down on a low wall halfway to the water's edge and began a water-colour painting of the bridge. Several of the huge dusty giants came and joined the little crowd that gathered curiously round me. After a few moments, when they realised what I was drawing, a lively conversation began and I could frequently pick out the word 'police'. Something jogged in my memory and I recalled being told that certain places in India, particularly airfields, railway stations and bridges, are not allowed to be photographed or drawn. One of the young body-builders spoke to me directly in his own language. I heard the word police and he mimed tearing up my sketch book.

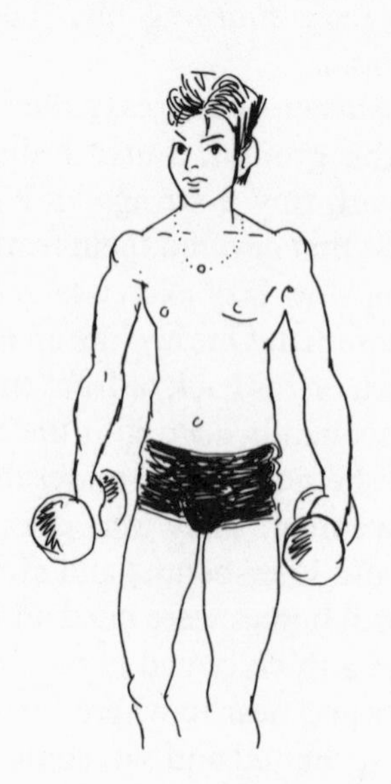

Body-builder, Calcutta

I felt if they all just went away no one would particularly notice me sitting quietly in the crowd, but as it was they were with their lively interest signalling clearly to any passing policeman what was going on.

I hurried my work and was not at all pleased with it. I also felt very angry with the stupid regulation about drawing the bridge; after all, every guide book contains photographs of it. On the other hand I was quite worried about being picked up by the police. They are some of the most scary-looking coppers I've ever seen and they have an appalling reputation. My white skin, I had been told, would mean they could be even more difficult than usual. 'They are often quite funny about foreigners.'

The young body-builder asked me to draw him and posed holding two dumb-bells and flexing his muscles.

I watched a bearded *sadhu* or holy man sitting under a makeshift shelter. Wreaths of marigolds lay on the ground in front of him and a woman appeared to be preparing food for him. A little boy entered the shelter and sat down. The holy man handed him some food and they both watched me watching them.

Sadhu under Howrah Bridge, Calcutta

An old man tied one end of a long piece of cloth to a post and stood holding the other end while it dried in the hot sun. I looked away and when I looked back he had gone, and an old woman was drying her sari in his place. Far away, on the further bank, I could just see more people washing and resting and moving to and fro.

I walked towards the bridge and went under the road that leads off it. There were stalls selling food and I saw a small girl sitting in front of a huge pile of prawns' heads and tails. They smelt strong and she was separating out some bits from others. I watched for a while but could not tell why she chose certain bits for one pile and threw away others.

I climbed some steps up to the bridge and joined the flow of people, allowing myself to be carried along back towards the city. The pedestrians overflowed the footpath and walked in

Fire engines, Calcutta

and out among the rickshaws and handcarts that jostled along the kerb. Cars and lorries and buses filled the centre lanes.

As I came off the bridge into the city I vaguely assumed the crush would disperse—but it didn't. I found myself swept along into an incredibly crowded street. Busy shops and stalls lined each side of the way and the pavements and road were solid with traffic and pedestrians. All the motor vehicles honked continuously and the rickshaw boys let out yelps and cries as they tried to force their way forward. I had to carry my bag held before me like a shield, because if it swung from my shoulder or I carried it at my side, it continually caught against other people and was nearly tugged from my grasp.

After fifteen minutes or so of trying to make headway in this extraordinary crush I found I had gone only a few hundred yards. I began to think that at this rate I would never get back to the Twites' by lunch-time. I also noticed that the motor traffic was not moving much faster than I was. It puzzled me a little that no one seemed angered by the crush. No one frowned or looked violent or appeared unduly frustrated by not being able to move.

I turned down an alley hoping to move across to an emptier street. The alley was as difficult to get down as the street I'd left and eventually brought me to another wide thoroughfare that was equally crammed. I was getting very hot, and rapidly tiring of this experience. I looked at the upper storeys of the buildings; behind filthy windows more people were getting on with the day. The city was full in a way I've never imagined a city could be; not just parts of it, but all of it; not just outside, but indoors as well.

More because I wanted to sit down than because I thought it would speed my journey I got into a taxi. Sometimes we moved forwards, sometimes we waited. Each time we came to a halt the driver switched off the engine, to save petrol I suppose. Two men opened the passenger door and then got into the front seat after a brief conversation with the driver. They took no notice of me and after riding for a few blocks they silently got out and disappeared into the crowd.

Calcutta

When we got nearer to the hotel the way cleared a little and I got to the Twites' in perfect time for lunch.

Their flat was cool and quiet. A servant showed me into a shaded balcony and brought me a fresh lime juice and soda. While I waited a girl in her twenties came and talked to me. She was very pretty and was wearing European clothes. She spoke extremely good English and told me she had worked for Mr Twite for some time.

She asked me about my travels and we fell to talking about dacoits. She said she would no longer take a train to Bombay or Delhi: it was too dangerous. The guards were useless against the dacoits and probably worked with them. To be in a women's compartment was more risky than being elsewhere in the train because Indian women always travel with lots of jewellery and the robbers always go straight to find them. Her brother still goes by train but she flies and considers the extra price well worth it.

When the Twites arrived the pretty girl disappeared although they urged her to stay and have a drink.

After lunch Mr Twite gave me the letter of authority I needed to get the medal and lent me his car and driver. Mrs Twite invited me to accompany her that evening to the opening of an exhibition of Bengal Art. It promised to include some Kalighat pictures and I accepted gratefully.

I swept up to the University in the grand car and the driver showed me where he'd wait. Mr Pal was waiting for me in his quiet musty office. He smiled and shook hands. After reading Mr Twite's letter he reached into a drawer and took out a box which he opened carefully. There was the solid gold medal and without further formalities he handed it to me. He explained that it had been very difficult to send the medal through the post because the insurance was so complicated and permission to export that much gold also hard to organise. I felt a little uneasy about how I was going to export it.

'So you see,' said Mr Pal, obviously relieved, 'your coming

here to get the medal is a godsend.'

He begged me to make sure my father-in-law acknowledged the medal immediately he got it, so that the file could be closed. '. . . and please give him my best wishes for a happy Christmas and New Year,' he said. The words fell oddly into the hot, still Indian air.

I put the medal in its box away into my pocket and asked Mr Pal if he could direct me to the University Art Gallery, where I knew there to be many Kalighat pictures. He came with me to the Gallery and introduced me to a professor of art history. In the corridor and in the office where we sat were a number of pictures and carvings. All were extremely dusty and grubby and could hardly be seen in the dim light. There seemed to be a delay because tea was brought and there was a lot of coming and going. I slowly realised that the Gallery was shut and could not be opened.

The kind and knowledgeable professor said he was sorry but at least I could take away a set of large coloured reproductions of Kalighat pictures that the Gallery had produced. He went away and returned a few minutes later smiling and shrugging.

'I'm sorry,' he said, 'it appears they are out of print.' I was disappointed, but also in a perverse way delighted by the hopelessness of it all. Nothing was happening, all activity was apparently suspended, time slowed down.

Mr Pal said goodbye and left and I thought I should go too. By the time I got back to the Twites I suddenly felt I was going to collapse. I was drained of energy and felt almost faint.

It wasn't the day that had tired me, it was the whole three weeks I'd been in India. This was my last evening in Calcutta and like a runner at the end of a race, I was exhausted.

Mrs Twite must have noticed I was looking grey, because she asked if I'd like to lie down in the guest room. I wondered how to get back to the hotel and began to dread going to meet Akbar at seven thirty, but I was too drained to work it all out. I slept for an hour or so and woke feeling a little better.

The exhibition was small and very badly hung and the room it was in was stiflingly hot and reeked of sickly-sweet joss-stick smoke, but pinned up with clothes-pegs and crudely mounted on card were some beautiful Kalighat paintings and drawings. I was relieved to find them; it would have seemed terrible to come to Calcutta and not see any.

I did not stay long. Outside it was very dark and it took me a moment to realise that not only had night fallen but no street lights had come on; most of the houses and buildings were in total darkness. There was obviously a power cut. It seemed to affect most of Calcutta. On the way back to Akbar's office the only light came from the headlights of cars and lorries.

I walked the last few hundred yards. The night was full of smoke from cooking fires and it was very dark.

Akbar was tired and not very communicative. I asked him why he lived in Calcutta rather than Delhi or Bombay for example. He said, 'Well, I was born here, but I stay because this is where my work happens to be. I'd work anywhere; I'd go to hell if the job was good enough.' He said there were several of his friends in town and he'd asked a few over to his flat.

We got into his car and set off to pick up one of his guests. A few yards away along the narrow road, two men were pushing a car that had clearly just broken down. Another car was trying to pass it by driving over the pavement. Our driver tried to do the same: in no time at all everything was hopelessly jammed up. Akbar swore. 'I am convinced,' he said moodily, 'no traffic jams are caused by accident. They are all deliberate and caused by sheer malice.' I couldn't quite see who he blamed for this incident. I felt our impatient driver was probably most at fault. I said something about the jam I'd been in that morning. 'Yeah,' said Akbar, 'you just have to remember. If you're travelling across Calcutta, take a book.'

We picked up the friend from his hotel. He works for an English publisher as their chief representative in India. Akbar cheered up a bit; he was obviously glad to see his friend.

At the flat Mallika had had a difficult day. Her eldest child is terribly jealous of the baby. 'She complained for two and a half solid hours this afternoon,' said Mallika.

'What did you do?' I asked.

'I tried not to get cross,' said Mallika. 'I try to tease her out of it. I tell her not to be silly. I finished up carrying her around.'

Someone mentioned the Gandhi film that had just opened. The publisher said he'd seen it. Akbar asked, 'What's it like?'

'It's *shit*,' said the publisher angrily, 'absolute shit.'

'Why? What's wrong with it?'

His answer was complicated. He had been infuriated by the sequence dealing with the massacre at Amritsar. He felt the British were whitewashed to an unforgivable degree. He quarrelled with much that had been left out and with the fact that historically it was full of errors with many people's importance wrongly depicted.

Akbar said scornfully that the makers of the film had given a Press conference which had been held in a simple room with no chairs—as a sort of self-consciously reverent gesture towards Gandhi's teaching and character.

'What rubbish,' he said.

Once when Robin Twite was mentioned the publisher exploded again. 'Do you know Twite?' he cried. 'He is a twit. Do you know what he told me? He told me the British Council in Calcutta had gone downhill. It had been allowed to become *too Indian*! If this had not happened in his house, I would have struck him.'

I don't know what on earth Twite had actually said but I couldn't help feeling there must have been a degree of misunderstanding in the conversation. But it was interesting nevertheless that the Indian had felt so insulted. He had, I gathered, not expressed his anger.

He railed on, half-laughing at his own rage. I found out myself a few seconds later how easy it is to put your foot in it. I mentioned going to the University to pick up the medal and laughingly described the place as a bit run down, saying not much seemed to be happening there. Akbar said coldly that he knew of several men who worked at the University whose dedication, scholarly ability and absolute integrity were second to none. He described one particular professor. 'I'm not the sort of man who touches peoples' feet when I meet them,' he said. 'I don't respect any man that much, except for him. I touch his feet.'

I had blundered. 'I didn't mean disrespect to any individual,' I said, embarrassed. I remembered Akbar saying, 'We get a lot of shit from British journalists telling us what is wrong with India.'

Several times when talking to Indians, I had noticed a prickly nationalist line in their attitude. They look for Indian solutions to Indian problems and are contemptuous of Mrs Gandhi's attempt to become a big international figure. I have the feeling they are inward-looking and even isolationist. Certainly they are pretty uninterested in England anyway, and to a degree in the opinions of English visitors or officials.

The flat was filling up with more people. All the late-comers were mildly tipsy. One was plastered. He said to me, 'I'm sorry; we will have no conversation this evening, you and I. I am far too drunk. Sorry.' He was wearing a tie with the same colours that are on the cover of the Oxford English Dictionary, so everyone called him 'Dictionary'.

Mallika begged him not to speak Hindi. 'His Hindi is so terrible it's awful to listen to,' she said to me, giggling.

All the newcomers were male and they all laughed and joked much of the time. They also tried to speak seriously sometimes. . . .

'As a civil servant, is my first loyalty to the government or to the constitution?'

'To the constitution of course, because . . .'

'No, no, but listen . . .'

'Be quiet, my dear sir, I'm answering your question.'

'My dear sir? who are you calling my dear sir . . .'

But in no time they were in fits of laughter again. I noticed that they all touched each other often, held hands when trying to make an important point or leaned affectionately together laughing. One man took my hand when trying to make me accept another whisky.

'Please,' he said, 'go on, have another.'

'Go on,' said Mallika.

As time went by I realised Akbar was not going back to the office tonight. I was starving hungry and terribly tired. I longed to be in bed. I said to Mallika, 'Perhaps I could get myself a taxi.'

'No,' she said, 'as soon as this power cut is over we'll eat, then Akbar's car will take you back.'

Several people began complaining about the power cut. It was an unusually bad one and was paralysing most of Calcutta. No trains were leaving or entering Howrah station, special squads of police were out to prevent law-breaking and many high-rise blocks were in turmoil with no lifts, no lights and cooking stoves out of action. I remembered with embarrassment my admiration for the Indian and his ghee lamp surviving the London power cut.

Mallika explained a conversation that was going on on the other side of the room. All through the evening she remained aware that I couldn't understand half the conversation and would murmur 'speak English, speak English,' as one or other of her guests broke into another language. Sometimes she translated for me what was going on.

'Those two men are Moslems, that one a Hindu,' she said pointing to a group round Akbar, 'the other I'm not sure. They are talking about Moslems being mistrusted. All Moslems are suspected of being allies of Pakistan. Akbar will never visit Pakistan because people would say, "See, he is one of them". Moslems therefore become extremely patriotic, more royalist than the King, forever establishing their loyalty.'

One man began telling a joke about the President of Pakistan. He spoke English for my benefit. The joke concerned a discussion about what should be inscribed on the President's tombstone and the punch line was 'commit no nuisance here'. At least, I think that's what he said; it produced helpless laughter.

Thus encouraged, the storyteller began another joke. This time it was about the wife of the President of Pakistan going to some official to say she wanted a divorce. On being asked why on earth she wanted to divorce so powerful, wonderful and important a man, she replied, 'Because he's doing to the country what he should be doing to me.' This was obviously an old joke (I've heard it before about other world leaders) because as the storyteller got to the punch line he was laughing so much in anticipation he could not speak, and one or two others, giggling hysterically, spoke the words for him. One man, the same who had held my hand earlier, toppled sideways and rolled over and over across the floor gasping and choking with laughter and repeating the joke to himself. The original storyteller spoke the punch line again in English and then in his own tongue in order to savour it more. Others tried different translations into English to improve the joke, if possible.

I laughed too, more at their laughter than at the joke itself.

The publisher spoke to me about his work and robustly criticised his head office in London. He said they were utterly stupid and out of touch with India's needs and the kind of taste they should cater for. 'There is so much they could do here, so much good, if only they promoted and sold the right books.'

'I suppose they are mainly concerned to sell as *many* as possible,' I said. 'Could you raise their sales, do you think?'

'Of course I could,' he cried, 'if they'd only listen. All the chairman is interested in is making a new contract for thousands and thousands of pounds with Harold Robbins or Freddie Forsyth; he couldn't care less about India.'

'Have you tried to explain all this to them?'

'Yeah, lots of times; they won't listen.' He sounded depressed.

At long last and even though as far as I could tell the power was still off, Mallika said supper was ready. Food had been laid out on a table in another part of the flat. We helped ourselves and perched where we could to eat. All except two of us ate with their fingers. The food was delicious: curried chicken, some other meat, vegetables and rice, all spicy and hot. There was also a sweet custard-like pudding made from curd.

After dinner there followed an interminable discussion about who was going home and how and who would stay with the Akbars. No one seemed to care one way or the other except me, who remained silent, and the publisher who was determined to get a lift from Akbar's driver. I attached myself to him. Several others tried to as well but Akbar told them they lived too far away as the car had almost no petrol in its tank.

We got into the hall and tried to call the lift. Some descended by stair to find the lift, others waited. In the end, after barely saying goodbye and thank you to the Akbars I found myself in the lift with the publisher and the big jolly storyteller. At about the fifth floor the lift was unexpectedly stopped. The door opened and Dictionary appeared. He grabbed the storyteller and pulled him out. Both disappeared chuckling and protesting and the publisher and I continued alone.

In the car he said to me seriously, 'Well, how are you going to describe this evening when you come to write it up?'

'I'll say there was a great deal of laughter and drinking and that the mood changed very quickly; that you are an extremely volatile lot, all solemn one moment and utterly frivolous and jokey the next.'

'What else?'

'That the food was terrific.'

'Umm.'

'I'll try to remember what people said. I'll describe Akbar as a serious, moody, even a rather troubled man, in spite of his cool tough manner.' I said this mainly to see if he'd agree.

'Yes, he is a very serious man,' was the reply. 'But didn't you notice,' he continued, 'that behind all the laughter and fooling about there is a great sadness?'

'No, I can't say I did notice that,' I admitted, rather surprised, 'but remember you were often talking in languages I could not understand and I could not pick up the nuances of your conversation.'

'Mmm,' he said thoughtfully.

'What causes this sadness?' I asked.

'We have many problems,' he replied, not making it clear

whether he meant the whole country or each as individuals. I had no time to question him further because we had arrived at his hotel.

We shook hands and he said it had been a pleasure to meet me and to talk. I said something similar and meant it very sincerely. He was a most interesting man, very friendly and good-humoured but also passionate and capable of bursts of considerable anger. At one time earlier in the evening, he had said to me that although he worked for a foreign company he felt he was helping India nevertheless, and did not feel bad or awkward about not being attached to an Indian concern. I had thought, how strange that he felt the need to explain that. He was a very proud man.

As he walked away from the car into the dark he half turned and waving his arm shouted something over his shoulder. It was a moment or two before I realised what he had said. 'Remember—*Twite is a twit*!' He was laughing again.

Friday 3rd December

My last day. I woke up weak with exhaustion and feeling a little hungover from last night. I have barely drunk any alcohol while I've been in India and last night's whisky affected me more than usual. I felt utterly fatigued. I'd done it and now all I had to do was get on an aeroplane and in a few hours I'd be back with my family.

I was terrified of missing the plane and checked and double-checked the departure time. I couldn't make the effort to go and do or see anything. Even my mind seemed to have collapsed. About lunch-time I went for a walk and discovered a large indoor market or bazaar near the hotel. Several boys wearing little red badges and carrying baskets badgered me to follow them.

'Don't go in there,' one said as I paused by a shop. 'Come with me.' I went in anyway and asked the shopkeeper who the boys were.

'They work in the market for certain merchants,' he said. 'If you accompany them all the prices will be higher, because the shopkeepers include their commission on anything you buy.'

'I gather they don't work for you.'

'No, I don't like them. From me all you pay is the fair price, no added commission,' he said. 'They have quite a strong union,' he added.

I liked the man. He said, 'Come and look at my other shop.' He locked up and led me through the market. One of the boys followed. 'Don't go with him, he is a bad man,' he hissed. I ignored him and so did the man.

Swimming pool,
Oberoi Grand Hotel, Calcutta

At the other shop I met my guide's father and brother. I was offered tea and given a chair. The brother lolled in a hammock and we talked in a lazy, friendly way. I bought two beautiful little dolls. Each was constructed of four parts, which when balanced correctly one on top of another, formed a sari-clad woman, who swayed and nodded and turned if you nudged or blew on her. They were beautifully painted, and made of papier-mâché, and cost five rupees each, or about thirty-five pence. They were very fragile and I asked for them to be carefully packed; an assistant wrapped each piece in newspaper and put them in a cloth bag for me to carry.

I couldn't shake off the sensation of sleepwalking. I sat for a long time by the swimming pool of the hotel and tried to think of something to do but felt content to rest in the shade and drink fresh lime and soda.

At the back of my mind I worried slightly about the gold medal, but there was nothing I could do about it: I just hoped the customs would not find it. Yesterday Akbar had asked me whether I'd got all the correct papers for exporting the great hunk of gold, and when I'd said no, he had whistled, pulled a face and said, 'Then go to the airport at least two hours early!'

I left for the airport in plenty of time. It was already getting dark and there was another power cut. The streets were very crowded and full of traffic. I was glad I was in no hurry. My driver was in a greater hurry than I as a matter of fact because he wanted to get back in time to watch, or listen to, an important hockey match due to start in an hour or so.

At the airport I waited with a few other early arrivals to check in. An Englishman nearby went through some papers; we nodded to each other. Over a loudspeaker it was announced that all passengers should go to a certain window to pay the hundred-rupee airport tax.

'Humph!' said the Englishman. 'That's a new one.'

I wasn't sure I had a hundred rupees left.

'I can lend you some,' he said cheerfully. It turned out I had just over a hundred rupees. I changed the rest and got about three pounds back.

When I checked in my luggage I was over the allowed weight but the clerk said I could carry one little extra bag with me.

The next check was customs.

'Have you anything to declare?'

'No.'

'Have you bought any jewellery; any silver or gold?'

'No,' I said, arguing to myself that I had not bought the gold I was carrying. I remembered that a little coral necklace I'd bought had some silver beads on it. I began to describe it.

'No, no, that's all right,' said the customs man and marked my bags.

While we waited outside security, I talked to the Englishman. He was a businessman who came to India two or three times a year, but he appeared to have relatively little contact with Indians other than the formal business meetings that his work demanded; and he'd seen very little of the country. He liked India though. He planned to bring his wife one day and explore a little. He asked if I had liked India and when I said that I had very much, he said, 'I can see that it's got you.' He smiled and quoted some words he thought came from Kipling. 'I can't remember it exactly,' he said, 'but the gist is "Some men hate India and cannot get away fast enough, but the rest die there".'

Jet planes have created a great number of men like this. They have travelled very widely but seen relatively little. This man had once been a sea captain and was not unadventurous, or incurious. He expressed envy at the number of people I had met and the places I'd been able to visit here.

We went into the security check together. My officer asked me to open my two bags. Actually I had three, because round my neck was slung my precious dolls in their cloth bag.

The officer asked me to open up the dolls. He looked amazed when I carefully undid the newspaper wrapping. To my horror I saw that the base of each doll was missing. The man who had packed them up so carefully had simply left them out. I flew into a ridiculous fury in my disappointment. I swore and stamped. I had been looking forward to showing them to

Caroline more than any of the other things I'd acquired. I had been so pleased to find them.

The officer said, 'We have a problem.' He pointed out firmly that I had three bags as hand luggage and that I was only allowed one. He looked casually in my shoulder bag in which I carried my drawing things, passport, tickets and the medal.

'You'll have to check one in,' he said. I protested because the clerk downstairs had told me I could carry the other bag, which was quite small, and anyway I had no money left to pay for any excess baggage. The officer insisted.

I became aware that the Englishman was having a blazing row right next to me. He had been stopped for the same reason. He was red in the face and beside himself with rage.

'I always carry these cases,' he bellowed. They both contained work things and were small. 'If you think they are a security risk, bloody search them. Search me. I'm taking them with me. I've had enough of your stupid bloody bureaucracy. I want to see your boss. I demand to see a British Airways Official.'

The Indian officers stared at him, completely unmoved.

'You can only take one with you. It's regulations.'

'Bugger regulations. You are just being idiotic.' But it didn't do the slightest bit of good. No high-up official appeared and the security men refused to change their minds, except to say that only first-class passengers were allowed more than one piece of hand-luggage. This information made the Englishman angrier than ever. 'So, it's not even a security thing,' he shouted. 'Do you suppose hijackers can't travel first class? How bloody daft can you get?'

This scene seemed to me a useful diversion from the medal so I protracted it for a bit and then agreed to go and check one of my bags through downstairs. The Englishman accompanied me. We arrived back at the check-in counter where the argument started again.

The chief official said wearily to his assistant, 'Check them through.'

'The trouble is,' said the clerk, pointing at me, 'he's already checked his luggage and this one is extra.'

I cursed him silently.

'Oh, never mind,' said the chief who was obviously bored with the whole thing. The assistant shrugged and smiled at me and took my bag. 'So far so good,' I thought and trailed off through customs back to the security stop.

'Is it O.K., can I go through now?' I called to my officer.

'No,' he said. 'I want to look in that bag.'

'Damn,' I thought.

I opened my satchel and he began going through it ridiculously carefully. He picked up bottles of ink and flicked through notebooks. Each time he dropped one of these bits, I'd replace it in the bag. I tried half-heartedly to keep the medal in its box hidden while I pretended to help him. He carefully and methodically continued to go through my things. At last he picked up the box with the medal in it.

'What's this?' he said.

'Oh, that belongs to my father-in-law,' I said irritably and completely meaninglessly. He dropped the box and nodded. I closed the bag and walked through the doorway to the left. Here a metal detector was passed over me and I was searched but allowed to go on.

A few moments later I was standing on the tarmac looking at the British Airways aircraft that was waiting for us. It had engines at the back and was not a jumbo 747.

'Oh God,' I said. 'Is that a DC10?'

'It's a Tristar,' said the Englishman, walking beside me.

An air hostess showed me to my seat. The Englishman waved and grinned. 'Have a good journey,' he said.